CONVEYANCING

CONVEYANCING

RECENT DEVELOPMENTS

Richard Hegarty, LLB,
Solicitor

OLD BAILEY PRESS

LAW IN PRACTICE SERIES

OLD BAILEY PRESS
200 Greyhound Road, London W14 9RY

© Richard Hegarty 1999

ISBN 1 85836 286 5

British Library Cataloguing-in-Publication Data

A catalogue record for this book is available from the British Library.

Printed and bound in Great Britain

Contents

Preface

Conveyancers have had a difficult time in the 1990s and there is no sign that the next millennium will be any better for them. There have been many statutory changes and landmark cases which conveyancers have had to contend with. I have covered both the important cases and the various statutes so that any conveyancers reading the book or using it for reference will have all the changes in the law and practice since 1994. I have tried throughout to explain the practical consequences of any changes on the life of a conveyancer.

I have included a chapter on the state of the conveyancing market at the present time. It is important for conveyancers to know their market and to anticipate the changes they will have to make in the next few years. I have also covered the Solicitors' Practice (Lender and Borrower) Amendment Rule 1998. This will limit the ever-increasing liability that conveyancers have had to face from the lenders and it is vital for any conveyancer to know the rule thoroughly.

The *Etridge* case which was reported as I was writing the book will present substantial problems for the conveyancer in years to come. I have set out in the book a checklist which I hope will be of practical use to all advising in this area.

I hope students, whether trying to qualify or those already qualified and endeavouring to keep up with the rapid pace of change in conveyancing, will find the depth in which I have dealt with the subject matter to their liking.

I would like to thank my family and colleagues for their help in writing this book.

Richard Hegarty
February 1999

Table of Cases

1 The Present Conveyancing Market

Introduction

Conveyancers often compare the present-day conveyancing market with the heady days of 1987/88. At that time there was a boom in conveyancing and the volume of transactions completed was at an all-time high. In July 1988, which some may remember as the month before the joint double tax relief was withdrawn, there were 212,000 conveyancing transactions. In July 1995 there were a mere 91,000 conveyancing transactions, which gives some idea of the extent of the subsequent collapse of the conveyancing market. The figure has since increased, but in July 1997 there were only 119,000 transactions, just over half the 1988 total.

It may seem senseless to an outsider to compare the conveyancing market of today with that of 1988. The recession in conveyancing, however, has brought about other fundamental changes, some of which are only just beginning to affect conveyancers – it has probably delayed by five years institutions coming into conveyancing. There has been little or no profit in the sector since 1990 and only the resurgence of the housing market in 1997 has created interest from non-solicitor institutions who now realise that the profit may be coming back into the market.

The boom of 1987 and 1988 has had other repercussions. It has led to a mass of claims, both by private clients and by lending institutions in relation to conveyancers' negligence. There is no doubt that the quality of some conveyancing carried out in the late 1980s was appalling. Throughout the 1990s there had been a steady increase in the amount that the Solicitors Indemnity Fund has paid out due to solicitors' negligence relating to conveyancing. Some claims related to responsibilities that no conveyancer could have foreseen in the late 1980s, but many arose from sloppy conveyancing, brought about by the desire of conveyancers to undertake whatever volume of work presented itself. There is no doubt that during this period conveyancing was carried out by people who did not have the necessary expertise and training. The profession has paid dearly for these mistakes.

The 1990s has also seen an increase in influence of the large lending institutions on the conveyancing market. Although not directly involved in the conveyancing process, their dominance in the market-place has enabled them to dictate terms to conveyancers and created a situation whereby the conveyancing profession now effectively indemnifies against much of the bad lending practice that was seen in the late 1980s and early 1990s.

The improvement of the quality of conveyancing

In 1990 the Law Society launched 'Transaction' which introduced the Standard Conditions of Sale to be used in all residential conveyancing. The protocol provided for the seller to provide as much information about a property as possible, and to warrant that information, thus, hopefully, reducing the number of enquiries a conveyancer would have to make. It was envisaged that this protocol would improve efficiency, reduce the time taken to complete a transaction and generally improve the quality of conveyancing. Conveyancers were rather slow to adopt the new procedure. It is now used, however, widely and successfully throughout England and Wales.

There is no doubt that the quality of conveyancing has improved considerably over recent years. This is evidenced by the substantial increase in pre-contract enquiries that are made now, even within routine residential conveyancing. Most conveyancers send a detailed report to the client before exchange of contracts and are encouraged to go through the report with the client and explain the whole process. There is less room for misunderstanding by the purchaser and more likelihood that any inherent defects in the property will come to light before the exchange of contracts. There has also been a realisation on the part of conveyancers that lenders are as equally important as borrowers and their interests must also be protected.

Current changes taking place in the conveyancing market

The computer

It is no longer possible to profit from conveyancing unless new technology is embraced. In the past, conveyancers answered post and draft contracts and transfers via a dictating machine. A secretary would type what was produced. There would be continual interruptions as clients and other conveyancers rang to chase matters. The whole process was very labour-intensive and costly. The computer has enabled automation of parts of the conveyancing procedure. Many support packages provide for data to be input once and then to be used continually in the generation of letters, contracts, transfers and other documents. Parts of the work can be delegated to so-called paralegals who are properly supervised and supported by qualified staff. This reduces the cost of each conveyancing transaction. It also speeds up procedures and the client can be given updated information regularly as to progress. It can, however, de-personalise the whole process. The computer enables anyone in the office to report to a client on the up-to-date position; this often means that a client will speak to two or three different people and will not really know who is dealing with the matter. However, if used properly it does reduce the risk of mistakes. It is inevitable that there will be greater dependence on the computer if the quality of conveyancing continues to improve.

Research carried out in early 1998 by the Law Society has shown that England and Wales has the cheapest conveyancing process in Europe. It is, however, the slowest and many clients will happily accept the introduction of technology if it means that they can move into their houses sooner.

Licensed conveyancers

Solicitors have 96 per cent of the conveyancing market. Licensed conveyancers have 2 per cent of the market and the balance is made up of people who act for themselves. There are some 300 Licensed Conveyancers holding full licences, but there are over 800 Licensed Conveyancers in training and there is no doubt that solicitors will continue to lose some of their market share to Licensed Conveyancers over the next few years. In 1997 Hambro Countrywide obtained a waiver from the Council of Licensed Conveyancers, which enabled them to carry out conveyancing for the clients of Hambro Countrywide Estate Agency. Other institutions may follow this example. Hambro Countrywide Conveyancing has a number of regional centres to which buyers and sellers will be introduced. They will not act for both seller and buyer and have indicated that as a matter of policy they will not deal with leasehold matters. There is a standard fee for any consideration of £350 plus VAT and disbursements. There has also been an increase recently in the number of arrangements that some firms of solicitors have with estate agents for the introduction of work through the Introduction and Referral Code. All these changes will have a marked effect on the conveyancing process over the next few years.

Property selling

Solicitors have been able to sell properties for many years but their governing professional rules were very restrictive and few succeeded in combining both the selling of property and conveyancing. In 1997 the Law Society substantially relaxed the rules regulating property selling. Their strategy is based on the premise that solicitors need to be the first point of contact in house-selling and purchase and it will enable direction to be given as to who undertakes the conveyancing. If estate agents or lenders practise conveyancing then it is likely they will persuade clients to let them deal with their conveyancing in-house. Solicitors will find it increasingly difficult to compete with one-stop shopping and although there will still be a market for independent solicitor conveyancers, volume business will flow to estate agents and lenders if they deal with substantial segments of conveyancing.

Solicitors are now able to sell property in a number of different ways. There is, no doubt, a realisation on their part that if they are to retain a substantial proportion of the conveyancing market, they will have to become involved in property selling either individually, or with other firms of solicitors. A new Rule 6 of the Solicitors' Practice Rules came into force on 16 January 1998. The Solicitors' Publicity Code 1990 has also been amended to allow solicitors to advertise a composite fee for property selling and conveyancing services which is lower than the sum of the two separate fees. The changes are summarised below.

- Selling property through a solicitors' practice.

  This has always been possible, but the previous rule – forbidding a solicitor property seller from acting for both seller and purchaser even where the Rule 6 exceptions applied – has now been abolished. The solicitor property seller is now able to sell financial services and mortgage products to any buyer who comes into his office. Informed consent is required from all parties.

- Joint property selling by more than one firm of solicitors.

  The same rules apply as when solicitors sell through an individual practice, as above.

- Solicitors' property centres

  A 'SEAL' is a Solicitor Estate Agency Limited that does not undertake conveyancing and is jointly owned by at least four firms of solicitors, none having a controlling interest. It must operate from accommodation physically divided from and clearly differentiated from that of any participating practice. The emphasis of the new rules has been to encourage solicitors to join together in a particular locality and sell property through a SEAL. The competitive advantages of such arrangements are substantial and provide realistic opportunities to compete successfully with estate agents and institutions that provide both property selling and conveyancing. The SEAL is able to act for the seller and have one participating firm do the conveyancing for the seller and another participating firm do the conveyancing for the buyer. There are requirements to disclose to both parties the involvement of participating firms and to obtain the informed consent of the clients.

* Hived-off estate agency

  Solicitors can now own a hived-off estate agency, regulated by the Estate Agents Act 1979. Before the recent relaxation, it was not possible for a solicitor to act for the buyer or seller if he had an interest in a hived-off estate agency. He can now act in that situation.

It remains to be seen whether solicitors will make use of the deregulation.

Number of conveyancing transactions

It is estimated that in 1997 there was a 13 per cent increase in the number of homes that were sold in England and Wales. There were approximately 1,436,000 homes that changed ownership. This compares with 1,266,000 in 1996. There is no doubt that there has been a slight upturn in the volume of conveyancing transactions, and this trend is likely to continue over the next two years. Interest rates have probably reached their peak and should now start to reduce providing a further incentive to buy property.

The price of homes

The surveys conducted by the Halifax on property price regularly make the headlines and in 1997 they showed that throughout England and Wales prices rose by 6.1 per cent. The Halifax index records, however, reveal considerable regional variations. In Greater London the index increased by 16 per cent. In Yorkshire and Humberside it increased by only 1.8 per cent. Full details of the percentage increases for different regions are set out overleaf.

Halifax index of property prices by region, 1997 (1996=100)

Halifax Regional Property Price Increases 1997 on 1996	
England and Wales	6.1
Greater London	16.0
Rest of South East	10.7
South West	7.5
East Anglia	6.7
East Midlands	5.8
West Midlands	5.6
Wales	3.1
North West	2.9
North	2.3
Yorkshire and Humberside	1.8

Conveyancing fees

The increases in property prices and conveyancing transactions in 1997 were not matched with an increase in conveyancing fees. In that year the average fee paid by buyers was £295 compared with £288 in 1996, an increase of 2.6 per cent as against the 1997 rise in the retail price index of 3.6 per cent. These figures conceal some regional variations. In the South East, the Midlands and the North West, average conveyancing fees actually fell in 1997 – 62 per cent of buyers paid less than £300 for their conveyancing that year. Surprisingly the greatest increase in conveyancing fees was recorded in Yorkshire and Humberside which conversely had the lowest property price increases.

Conveyancing fees at this level are not sustainable. Smaller firms who depend on conveyancing for a large percentage of their turnover are not surviving. The conveyancing profession generally cannot cover its costs at present fee levels.

From September 1998 the average premium payable by solicitors for professional indemnity will be £150 per conveyancing transaction. Clearly those firms charging well below £300 for each transaction cannot make a profit.

Average Conveyancing Fees in 1997
(Excluding VAT and Disbursements)

| | All Homes | | [By price, 1997] | | | |
	1996	1997	Under £30,000	£30,000 £49,999	£50,000 £74,999	£75,000 over
All transactions	288	295	220	255	287	364
Greater London	361	351	273	315	327	384
Rest of South East	321	316	259	279	294	350
South West	327	328	266	288	294	382
East Anglia	283	311	235	256	292	427
East Midlands	283	272	222	246	283	347
West Midlands	284	283	210	241	265	373
Wales	261	266	229	250	276	299
North West	299	282	215	254	304	377
North	211	224	182	210	230	306
Yorks & Humberside	240	271	208	243	305	412
Type of Home						
Detached	363	352	266	281	285	375
Semi-detached	263	273	205	245	275	329
Terraced	246	263	218	245	288	346
Flat	297	309	244	289	308	410
Bungalow	315	324	220	266	307	380
Whether first-time buyer						
First-time purchase	248	261	216	245	273	331
Other	324	326	229	275	300	374

The remortgage market reduced considerably in 1997 compared with 1996 and the fall was sufficient to offset increases in income from residential conveyancing resulting from the general improvement in the housing market. In general terms the remortgage market halved in 1997. No doubt this is a consequence of the increase in fixed-rate mortgages in preceding years and the accompanying penalties for redeeming mortgages within certain time limits.

A profile of conveyancers

In January 1998 the Law Society conducted a survey of solicitors to gather information on the type of work carried out in private practice; 28 per cent said that they practised conveyancing and 12 per cent of total fee-earning time was spent on this. The table below shows the relative importance of conveyancing by size of firm.

Importance of Conveyancing by Size of Firm				
	Total solicitors practising conveyancing	% of solicitors practising conveyancing	% of total fee-earning time spent on conveyancing	% of total gross fee income from conveyancing
All firms	15,553	28	12	11
Sole practitioner	2,689	49	26	22
2–4 partners	7,068	50	19	23
5–10 partners	3,402	31	15	18
11–25 partners	984	12	6	11
26+ partners	1,410	8	3	2

The table overleaf confirms anecdotal evidence that few younger solicitors coming into the profession are undertaking conveyancing.

A General Summary of Conveyancers		
	All solicitors in private practice	All solicitors practising conveyancing
Total	58,378	15,553
Gender	%	%
Men	70	75
Women	30	25
Age		
Under 35	44	12
35–44	25	32
45–54	24	35
55+	7	21
Size of firm	%	%
Sole practitioner	10	17
2–4 partners	25	45
5–40 partners	19	23
11–25 partners	14	7
26+ partners	31	8

Further reading

All data included in chapter 1 was obtained from the Law Society's Research and Policy Planning Unit's *Research Paper 2* entitled 'Conveyancing' and an update issued in 1998 entitled 'The Conveyancing Market Trends – Statistics and Research Findings as at April 1998'. The author is indebted to John Jenkins of the Law Society's Research and Policy Planning Unit for his assistance in preparing Chapter 2.

'Compete or co-operate'. John Jenkins. *Law Society Gazette*, 11 June 1997, p18

2   Insolvency (No 2) Act 1994

Introduction

This Act came into force on 26 July 1994 and was introduced to remedy what were perceived as errors in the drafting of the Insolvency Act 1986. If there had been a gift or a transaction at an undervalue, s339 of the 1986 Act gave the court powers on the application of the trustee in bankruptcy to set aside the transaction should the donor become bankrupt within five years after the date of the undervalue transaction. Section 342 of the 1986 Act provides some protection in certain circumstances against the use and power of s339 but this proved far too restrictive. Deeds of gift blighted titles and it was necessary to take out indemnity insurance. It was not only those that had benefited from the undervalue transactions, but also those that had subsequently acquired in good faith and for value by way of a genuine open market purchase that were at risk. Section 1 of the 1994 Act deals with setting aside transactions by companies which become insolvent and s2 deals with transactions by individuals who become bankrupt. The Act restores the position that applied under the Bankruptcy Act 1914 so that a subsequent purchaser would not be at risk from a transaction being set aside unless the purchaser had notice of the actual or potential bankruptcy of the original owner at the date of the completion.

The law

Section 339 of the Insolvency Act 1986 provides that gifts or transfers at an undervalue where consideration is paid to a third party can be set aside:

- if the transferor has a bankruptcy petition presented within a two-year period; or
- within a five-year period if the transferor was insolvent at the date of the transfer or became insolvent as a result of making it.

The five-year problem could be resolved by entering into a Declaration of Insolvency. This does not, however, assist if the transferor has a bankruptcy petition presented within two years of the transfer. If the transfer is in favour of an associate – which means a spouse, a relative, a partner, relatives of partners, employer or employee – then there is a presumption of insolvency from the date of the transfer unless the contrary can be proved.

Section 343(2) of the Insolvency Act 1986 states that:

> 'An order shall not prejudice any interest in property which was acquired by any person (other than a party to the transaction) in good faith, for value and without notice of the relevant circumstances.'

The problem arose over the inclusion of the words 'without notice of the relevant circumstances'. If the purchaser had notice of the gift or transfer at an undervalue then he was deemed to have notice of the relevant circumstances and there was no protection for that purchaser.

The effect of the Insolvency (No 2) Act 1994

The Act removes the requirement that a purchaser must not have notice of the circumstances. The amended provision is as follows:

> 'An order under ss339 or 340 (ss238 or 239 when dealing with insolvent companies) may affect the property of, or impose an obligation on, any person whether or not he is the person with whom the individual in question entered into the transaction or, as the case may be, the person to whom the preference was given; but such an order –
>
> a) shall not prejudice any interest in property which was acquired from a person other than that individual and was acquired in good faith and for value or prejudice any interest deriving from any such interest, and
>
> b) shall not require a person who received a benefit from the transaction or preference in good faith, for value and without notice of the relevant circumstances to pay a sum to the trustee of the bankrupt's estate, except where he was a party to the transaction or the payment is in respect of a preference given to the person at a time when he was a creditor of that individual.

A purchaser (in this context it includes any acquirer of an interest) will have protection provided:

- he buys for value;
- he has acquired the property in good faith;

Section 1(2) in the case of companies and s2(2) in the case of individuals defines more clearly when an interest is not acquired in good faith. If the purchaser has notice of both the surrounding circumstances, which means the existence of a Deed of Gift, or of the transfer at an undervalue and the relevant proceedings, which means the notice of the issue of the bankruptcy petition or the actual bankruptcy, then he will not be a purchaser in good faith. Notice of the surrounding circumstances and the bankruptcy proceedings will include actual knowledge, constructive notice or imputed notice.

It is important to appreciate that the notice must be both of the surrounding circumstances and the relevant proceedings. A purchaser who knows of the gift but has a clear bankruptcy search is therefore protected. If it is registered land and the conveyancer knows of the gift and the name of the donor then a bankruptcy search should be carried out against the donor.

Checklist when Deed of Gift or Transfer at Undervalue		
If land registered	Nothing on land registry title and nothing with pre-registration deeds	No action necessary
	Notice of gift or transfer at an undervalue	Make land charges search
	Land charges search does not show bankruptcy entry	No action necessary
	Land charges search shows bankruptcy entry	Purchaser has no protection if gift or transfer at undervalue within 5 years
If land unregistered	No gift or transfer at under-value within last 5 years	No action necessary
	Title shows gift or transfer at undervalue within the last 5 years	Make land charges search
	Land charges search does not show bankruptcy entry	No action necessary
	Land charges search shows bankruptcy entry	Purchaser has no protection if gift or transfer at undervalue within 5 years

If the land is registered and the gift took place before the 1994 Act came into force there may in some land registry titles be an entry in the register referring to the possibility of the gift being set aside under the Insolvency Act 1986. A bankruptcy search should be carried out against the donor and if clear when submitted with a subsequent transfer the Land Registry should delete the entry.

The Law Society's counsel's opinion

As soon as the 1994 Act came into force there was concern that it had not resolved the problems created by the 1986 Act. The Law Society obtained counsel's opinion from Gabriel Moss QC. He dealt with four questions that were still of concern to the conveyancing practitioner.

1 What is the effect of the dual notice exception on the subsequent purchaser on the open market from the undervalue transferee and also any further purchaser who later acquires on the open market from that person?

  • A transfers a property to B at an undervalue.

    B sells on the open market to C who buys in good faith.

    C knew of the undervalue transaction between A and B but at the time C bought there was no bankruptcy.

    C sells to D by which time bankruptcy proceedings have begun against A.

    D knows of the previous undervalue transaction.

    Is D open to proceedings under s339 Insolvency Act 1986?

    Counsel advised that D would not be open to such proceedings. He said that the underlying purpose of the legislation is to protect the bona fide buyer in good faith and for value while preventing creditors being cheated.

2 What does notice of a previous undervalue transaction and notice of bankruptcy proceedings actually mean?

  • Counsel advised that actual notice is relevant in these circumstances. When a conveyancer is dealing with unregistered title there may be notice on the title of either a transaction at an undervalue or a bankruptcy entry on a land charges search. This is sufficient notice. When dealing with registered title the only notice is from information contained on the title. Counsel suggests, however, that where a prospective buyer has notice of a previous transaction at an undervalue even though it is registered land, a land charges bankruptcy search is carried out against the undervalue transferor. This would rebut any presumption of bad faith.

3 What is the effect of the 1994 Act on mortgagees?

  • Counsel advised that the mortgagee's position is exactly the same as the acquirer of any other kind of interest. The mortgagee clearly acquires that interest for value and in good faith and is therefore protected under the terms of the Act. If a property is transferred subject to a mortgage and at an undervalue then no s339 problems arise as the mortgage agreement was entered into before the undervalue transaction took place.

4 Where A transfers property at an undervalue to himself and B jointly or A and B transfer to A or B alone does the protection afforded by the 1994 Act operate in relation to C, the subsequent acquirer?

- Counsel advised that C is protected in the same way as any other purchaser. The reasoning behind this is that when C purchases from A and B in good faith and for value, C acquires A's beneficial interest which has not been the subject of an undervalue transaction and B's beneficial interest which has been but which C does not acquire from 'that individual'. The interest acquired from A is outside s339 altogether and the interest acquired from B comes within the protection afforded by the 1994 Act. When A and B transfer jointly owned property to B, C will acquire from B and again will obtain the protection afforded by the 1994 Act.

Further reading

Law Society Gazette, 4 October 1995, Article on Insolvency (No2) Act 1994

3 Law of Property (Miscellaneous Provisions) Act 1994

Introduction

This Act makes provision for new covenants of title being implied on the disposition of a property and amends the law regarding dealings with property after the death of the owner. The Act came into force on 1 July 1995. It was felt by the Law Commission, which recommended the reform that the previous implied covenants for title were antiquated and convoluted, inflexible, did not give buyers what they required, and the limitation periods which applied were confusing.

The law

Section 2 sets out the covenants that are implied whether the disposition is expressed to be made with full-title guarantee or with limited-title guarantee. These are:

- That the seller has the right to dispose of the property. This extends beyond just the sale of freehold or leasehold and includes the granting of a lease or a right of way.
- That he will at his own cost do all that he reasonably can to give the buyer the title he purports to give. This includes ensuring the buyer is entitled to be registered as proprietor with at least the same class of title.
- Where the title to the interest is registered it shall be presumed that the sale is of the whole of that interest.
- If it is not registered and it is a leasehold interest it shall be presumed that the disposition is for the unexpired portion of the term of years created by the lease.

Section 3(1) sets out further implied covenants where the disposition is expressed to be with full-title guarantee. It is then implied that the disposition is free from all charges and incumbrances whether monetary or not and free from other rights exercisable by third parties other than any charges, incumbrances or rights which the seller does not and could not reasonably be expected to know about. Potential liabilities do not constitute any defect in title (s3(2)).

When a disposition is expressed to be with limited-title guarantee there is also an implied covenant that the seller has not since the last disposition for value created a charge or incumbrance which is still subsisting at the time of the disposition, or granted third-party rights over the property which are still subsisting at that time – or suffered the property to be so subjected, and that he is not aware that anyone else has done so (s3(3)).

Where the disposition is of leasehold land and is either made with full-title guarantee or with limited-title guarantee there will be an implied covenant that the lease is subsisting at the time of the disposition and that there is no subsisting breach of a condition or a tenant's obligation and that there is nothing that would render the lease liable to forfeiture (s4).

Section 5 implies covenants on the part of a mortgagor of land which is subject to a rentcharge, or of leasehold land. They are implied whether the disposition is with full or limited guarantee. If the property is subject to a rentcharge there is an implied covenant that the mortgagor will fully and promptly observe and perform all the obligations that are enforceable under the instrument creating the rentcharge (s5(2)). If the property is leasehold land, there is an implied covenant that the mortgagor will fully and promptly observe and perform all the obligations under the lease, which is subject to the mortgage, that are imposed on him in his capacity as tenant (s5(3)).

There is generally no liability under any implied covenants if the disposition is expressly made subject to a matter or if the recipient knew of the matter (s6). Section 7 provides that the benefit of the covenant runs with the land.

Section 14 of the Act amends the Administration of Estates Act 1925 and provides for the vesting of property in the Public Trustee where either the deceased died intestate or he died testate and there is no executor, or if there is an executor who ceased to be an executor before the grant of probate.

Section 15 amends the Land Charges Act 1972 and enables land charges that are created before the death of a person, pending land actions and writs and orders which would have been capable of registration but for the death, to be registered after the death. One important practical implication for the conveyancer is that the search period used when searching against a deceased person should not end on his death.

Section 16 amends s2(2) of the Administration of Estates Act and requires the agreement of all the personal representatives to contract and to convey an interest under a trust for sale of land. A service of a notice affecting land will be effective even if the owner has died, as long as the server of the notice has no reason to believe the owner is dead (s17). This does not apply to the Land Registry, a court or a tribunal. Section 18 provides for the service of notices if it is known or suspected the recipient is dead. It can be served addressed to the personal representatives at the last known address, and a copy sent to the Public Trustee.

The need to amend the implied covenants

There is often the need to amend the implied covenants in certain situations, drafting for which is as set out below.

- In a contract where provision must be made to amend the implied covenants:

  'The Seller will transfer the Property with full/limited title guarantee, but the transfer will contain provisions modifying any implied covenants as follows:'

- A very common exception is to provide for the sale to be subject to anything which is recorded in registers open to the public:

  'For the purposes of s6(2)(a) of the Law of Property (Miscellaneous Provisions) Act 1994 all matters now recorded in registers open to public inspection are to be considered within the actual knowledge of the transferee'

- When a personal representative transfers with limited-title guarantee s3(3) covenants that there have been no charges or incumbrances since the last disposition. A personal representative almost certainly will have had little or no knowledge of the property prior to the death and therefore needs to limit this implied covenant.

  'The covenant implied by s3(3) of the Law of Property (Miscellaneous Provisions) Act 1994 shall apply only so far as it relates to the actions or omissions of the Transferor since the death of the deceased'

- The same problem may arise where property is sold by trustees who are successors to the trustees who originally acquired the land. They would want to limit their liability for any deemed knowledge of their predecessors.

  'The covenant implied by s3(3) of the Law of Property (Miscellaneous Provisions) Act 1994 shall be varied so as to provide that none of the transferors shall be considered to be aware of an action of another person merely because it is or was known to or notice of it was given to a predecessor in title or a co-trustee'

- When leasehold land is transferred there is an implied covenant that there are no subsisting breaches of the tenant's obligations (s4(1)(b)). These obligations will almost certainly include repairing obligations which may not have been wholly complied with.

'The Transferor is not liable under any covenant implied by the Law of Property (Miscellaneous Provisions) Act 1994 for any breach of the terms of the registered lease concerning the condition of the premises comprised in the title above referred to'

- There will be the need to modify the same implied covenants when there is the grant of a sublease with full or limited title guarantee as the intermediate landlord gives the same implied covenant that there are no subsisting breaches of the tenant's obligations.

'The Transferor is not liable under any covenant implied by the Law of Property (Miscellaneous Provisions) Act 1994 for any breach of the terms of the Head Lease dated etc concerning the condition of the property demised'

Further reading

'A New Deal on Covenants' – *Law Society Gazette* – 11 January 1995

'The Way Ahead on Covenants' – *Law Society Gazette* – 17 May 1995

Practice Advice Leaflet No 7: Implied Covenants – HM Land Registry

4   Environment Act 1995

Introduction

The Act is a substantial piece of legislation dealing with the creation of the Environment Agency and many miscellaneous matters relating to the environment. Part II deals with contaminated land and abandoned mines and is relevant to conveyancers. It will only come into force when statutory guidance has been laid before Parliament. It is likely that this aspect of the Act will not be enforced until at least April 1999. It is still, however, vital for conveyancers to know and understand the impact that the provisions relating to contaminated land will have on the conveyancing process and on the conveyancer's liability. At the present time all the different players in the conveyancing process are desperately trying to pass responsibility for contaminated land to someone else. Lenders want to ensure that they are protected if their security is in doubt because of contaminated land and valuers want to ensure that they are not held to be responsible if contamination is discovered. It could be, therefore, that over the next decade, as in the past, conveyancers will be held responsible by the courts. It is vital that conveyancers understand their potential liability at this stage, even before Part II of the Environment Act 1995 is implemented.

The law

Section 78A defines contaminated land as:

> 'Any land which appears to the Local Authority in whose area it is situated to be in such a condition, by reason of substances in, on or under the land, that –
>
> a) significant harm is being caused or there is a significant possibility of such harm being caused: or
>
> b) pollution of controlled waters is being or is likely to be caused.

Substances

The condition of the land must result from substances either in, on or under the land. Substance can mean a natural or artificial substance whether in solid or liquid form or in the form of a gas or vapour. The substances can be in a building, on the land or in water which covers the land.

Significant Harm

This is likely to include:

Death, serious injury, cancer or other diseases, genetic mutation, birth defects or the impairment of reproductive functions.

Harm which is irreversible or where there is other substantial adverse change in the function of any living organism or ecological system notified as a protected site under relevant legislation.

Death, disease or other physical damage to property in the form of livestock or other owned animals, of wild animals which are the subject of shooting or fishing rights, or of crops.

Property in the form of buildings such that there is a structural failure or substantial damage to the extent that the buildings can no longer be used for the purposes intended.

Identification of contaminated land (s78B)

Local Authorities will inspect the area from time to time and identify any contaminated land and identify any areas which are seriously contaminated and require such land to be designated as a Special Site. Local Authorities will act in accordance with guidance which has yet to be issued but if it is ascertained that there is any contaminated land in their area then notice will be given to the Environment Agency, the owner of the land, any person who appears to be in occupation of whole or part of the land and any person who, under s78F, is deemed to be an appropriate person.

There is provision under s78C for the designation of Special Sites. These would generally be where the Environment Agency is likely to have the necessary expertise to deal with them and where contamination is serious rather than merely significant.

Service of Remediation Notice

Section 78D provides that either the Environment Agency or the Local Authority, once having identified any contaminated land, shall serve a remediation notice on the appropriate person, specifying what that person is to do by way of remediation and the timescale within which the work is to be done. There is provision under this section for notices to be served on more than one person, in which case the notice will state the proportion of the cost that each person is liable to bear. The notice need not necessarily state exactly what actions need to be taken and might only state the objectives which are to be achieved, leaving it up to the persons served with the notice to work out how the objectives would best be achieved.

Section 78F defines how to determine who the appropriate person is to bear responsibility for the cost of cleaning up the land. The section provides a checklist of likely persons.

Primary responsibility will fall on the person who caused or who knowingly permitted the contamination.

If it can not be discovered who caused the contamination, then the owner or occupier at the time of the Notice is the appropriate person. An owner is defined as

'A person (other than a mortgagee not in possession) who, whether in his own right or as trustee for any other person, is entitled to receive the rack rent of the land, or, where the land is not let at a rack rent, would be so entitled if it were so let'

Lenders other than those in possession are therefore specifically excluded from liability. There could still be repercussions for lenders who find themselves in possession because the borrower has abandoned the property and sent the keys to the lender. A lender would also be reluctant to take possession of land with the intention of selling it to recover a loan if a Remediation Notice had already been served. And, as soon as a lender was in possession it could then be served with a notice and find itself liable to remedy the contamination.

Section 78M sets out the penalties for not complying with a Remediation Notice. Failure to comply is an offence with a maximum fine of £5,000 and a daily penalty of £500. In the case of industrial, trade or business premises the maximum fine is £20,000 with a daily penalty of £2,000.

Practical implications for conveyancers

The first responsibility of the conveyancer will be to ascertain whether a Remediation Notice has been served. That question must be asked in all Preliminary Enquiries. It is by no means certain that local searches will disclose the existence of Remediation Notices. They will certainly not disclose land that is likely to be contaminated. If the form of the Local Search is not changed to provide for notification of the existence of a Remediation Notice then the conveyancer must enquire both with the Local Authority and the Environment Agency whether such a Notice has been issued and whether to their knowledge one is likely to be issued.

Planning permissions must be checked very carefully to see whether they contain any conditions which relate to contaminated land.

If a survey has been carried out by the buyer this must be checked carefully to see whether the surveyor has mentioned the possibility of contaminated land and in some way passed on responsibility to the conveyancer for ascertaining whether any contamination exists.

The buyer's mortgage conditions must be checked carefully to ensure that there is no specific reference to contaminated land and any responsibility placed on the conveyancer to make specific checks. Conveyancers should specifically advise lenders in writing that they are unable to verify the assumptions concerning contaminated land and that their report on title is limited accordingly. The borrower must also be made aware that the valuer has made a number of assumptions which the conveyancer cannot be expected to verify.

In drafting a lease of land, the conveyancer must pass on as much responsibility on to the tenant with regard to liabilities for contaminated land.

Conveyancers should consider making enquiries to public bodies other than the Environment Agency and the Local Authority. The Environmental Health Department, the Health & Safety Executive, the County Authority and the Planning Authority may have information relating to contaminated land. The Environmental Regulations 1992 established a positive right that any person seeking information on the environment could obtain it from any public body holding it. The information must be made available within two months. There are certain exceptions to public bodies being obliged to provide the information but any refusal must be explained in detail to the applicant.

Transferring liability

When the regulations come into force it may be possible for the seller's conveyancer when preparing the contract, to pass on the responsibility to the buyer of the land. Where a payment is made for remediation that forms part of the contract for the transfer of the ownership of the land, and the buyer specifically agrees to meet the cost of carrying out the remediation, or if there is a reduction in the purchase price specifically provided for in the contract to cover the cost of remediation, then the seller can avoid liability. Similarly, if the land is sold with a clear disclosure to the buyer as to the presence of pollutants and these have been taken into account in agreeing a price, then the seller avoids any further liability under the Act. It has also been suggested in draft guidance that in transactions between large commercial organisations where the seller has given the buyer permission to carry out his own survey this should normally be taken as sufficient indication that the buyer has knowledge of the contaminated land.

It is vital that conveyancers understand the basic process under which land is designated as contaminated in order that they can fully appreciate their responsibilities over the next decade in respect of buying and selling land generally. The existence of a Remediation Notice is not the conveyancer's only concern. The conveyancer must make reasonable enquires as to whether there is likely to be any possibility of contamination which might lead to a Remediation Notice.

The Royal Institution of Chartered Surveyors – contamination and its implications for chartered surveyors

It is important for conveyancers to be aware of the extent to which chartered surveyors and indeed valuers generally will want to remove their liability for the consequences of contaminated land. The guidance issued by the Royal Institution of Chartered Surveyors is extremely important and it is hoped that the Law Society will follow this lead very quickly and give detailed guidance to conveyancers. It is likely as a result that all surveyors' reports will now contain sufficient exclusions to ensure that the surveyor will not be liable if it is subsequently discovered that the land is contaminated. It is important that conveyancers similarly exclude their own liability. They have an obligation to make enquiries and an obligation to explain to their client what they have done. That should be the limit of their responsibility. It is important that the conveyancers make suitable provision now, even before the relevant part of the Act comes into force.

Radon

Radon is a natural, radioactive gas present in subsoil that can permeate buildings and expose the occupants to high radiation levels. Health studies have linked exposure to radon to an increased risk of lung cancer. Radon is measured in units of becquerels per cubic metre of air (Bq m³) and the average concentration in UK homes is 20 Bq m³. The level at which action is necessary is 200 Bq m³. The National Radiological Protection Board (NRPB) and the government recommend that householders should take action to reduce radon to at least below the level of 200 Bq m-3 and then to as low a level as possible.

Radon levels in homes are measured using two small plastic detectors which must be left in place for three months. Purchasers are not therefore normally able to obtain a measurement before deciding to proceed with a purchase. The NRPB have carried out a nationwide survey and have identified areas where 1 per cent or more of houses are likely to exceed the action level of 200 Bq m^3. In those parts of the country that have recorded high levels of radon, the building regulations require radon protective measures to be incorporated in the construction of new dwellings.

What action has to be taken by conveyancers?

- If it is known that the property is in a high-risk area enquiries must be made of the seller to see if radon has ever been measured. The buyer must be advised of the reply and, if necessary, the preventive measures that may be required. The buyer should be advised to have radon levels measured as soon as they take possession.
- If it is not known whether the property is in a high risk area the additional Question 36 on the local search form should be asked. The buyer's survey may also contain information as to whether the property is in a high-risk area.

Further reading

The Royal Institution of Chartered Surveyors 'Contamination and Its Implications for Chartered Surveyors – A Guidance Note', published by RICS Business Services Limited.

'Making a clean job of leasing', Nicholas Whitehead and Nadeem Khan, *Estates Gazette*, 8 February 1997

5 Trusts of Land and Appointment of Trustees Act 1996

The Trusts of Land and Appointment of Trustees Act 1996 (TOLATA) came into force on 1st January 1997. It is an important Act for conveyancers to understand. They often create trusts and perhaps do not appreciate fully their effect. The Act reforms the law on trusts of land and appointment of trustees. Strict settlements under the Settled Land Act 1925 will not be permitted in future. The doctrine of conversion has been abolished and statutory trusts for sale converted into trusts of land. The Act confers new powers and duties on trustees of land.

The law

Section 1 of the TOLATA defines trusts of land as any trust of property which consists of or includes land, including a trust created or arising before the commencement of the TOLATA. It may be an express, implied, resulting or constructive trust. It may be a bare trust, where the trustee is simply the nominee of the beneficiary owner. Because it affects all trusts that existed on 1st January 1997 the legislation is in that respect retrospective.

Section 2 prohibits the creation of any new settlements under the Settled Land Act 1925.

Section 3 purports to abolish the doctrine of conversion although it does no such thing. It does prevent the doctrine from operating in the case of a trust. A beneficial interest in land is no longer to be treated as an interest in the proceeds of sale but rather as an interest in the land itself. Beneficiaries therefore have an interest in the land itself and have rights of occupation, and a right to be consulted and have their wishes taken into account.

The power to postpone the sale cannot be excluded (s4). All trusts of land now have an implied power to retain the land even where previously there was an express trust for sale as well as a power to sell. The duty to sell which was formerly paramount is replaced by a more evenly balanced situation where the obligation to sell land is no stronger than the obligation to retain land (s5).

Section 6 sets out the powers of the trustees when dealing with the land.

25

There is a specific power to partition it with the consent of beneficiaries who are of full age and absolutely entitled in undivided shares (s7).

The powers can be excluded or restricted unless it is a charitable, ecclesiastical or public trust (s8). The powers of trustees are considerably increased and, in particular, they have the right to raise the purchase price of land by mortgage.

Section 9 sets out new rights for the trustees to delegate their powers or functions to a beneficiary in possession. These powers cannot be expressly excluded in the trust wording. The delegation is carried out by way of a power of attorney. The trustees would still have to issue a receipt for any capital moneys raised on a sale. In practical terms this would mean that a beneficiary with a power of attorney could contract to sell, but the trustee would need to join in the transfer. Any one trustee can revoke the attorney at any time.

Section 11 imposes a duty on the trustees of land to consult beneficiaries of full age who are beneficially entitled before exercising their powers. Beneficiaries with an interest in possession have a right to occupy the land if the purposes of the trust include making the land available for their occupation or the land is held by the trustees to be so available (s12). These rights can be excluded or restricted by an express revision in the trust. The trust may be liable to pay compensation to a non-occupying beneficiary (s13).

Section 14 repeals s30 LPA 1925. It enables a trustee of the land or any person with an interest in the property to apply to the court for an Order deemed fit in relation to the exercise by the trustees of their functions and the nature or extent of a person's interest in property subject to the trust. The jurisdiction is very wide and gives the court powers to define the extent of a cohabitee's interest, the right to occupy or any right of compensation. It has powers to adjudicate on disputes of the trustee's powers and it can injunct a sale if the beneficiaries' interests have not been taken into account. A mortagee can obtain a declaration of interest and a power of sale.

Section 15 sets out the matters to which the court will have regard in making an order. These include the settlor's intention, the purpose of the trust, the welfare of any children and the interests of any secured creditor of any beneficiary. No particular weight is given to any of these criteria.

Section 16 absolves the purchaser from the need to investigate whether there has been a breach of trust; therefore a purchaser does not have to investigate whether a trustee has had regard to the rights of the beneficiary or obtained the consent of the beneficiaries to a partition, or consulted with the beneficiaries.

Part II of the Act need not concern conveyancers directly and is more relevant to probate practitioners.

What this means to a conveyancer in practical terms

The terms of the usual trust clause in a conveyance or transfer need to be amended. The suggested new form where there is to be a beneficial joint tenancy is as follows:

> 'The Buyers shall hold the Property upon a trust of land for themselves as joint tenants beneficially so that the survivor of them is able to give a valid receipt for capital moneys arising out of a disposition of the property'

Conveyancers should consider restoring an obligation to sell as an overriding criteria in certain circumstances. Conveyancers must ask their joint purchaser clients what they want to happen if they fall out. This would be especially relevant if they are unmarried cohabitees. It would be negligent not to pose these questions to joint purchasers.

Conveyancers should in certain circumstances exclude the beneficiaries' right of occupation – for instance, where the property is being purchased as an investment or being put in joint names after a divorce and one spouse will not be living there.

Conveyancers can consider whether there should be an obligation in the trust to delegate their powers to a beneficiary in possession.

There is no need to extend the powers of co-owners to those of an absolute owner as this is done automatically in s6.

Conveyancers acting for purchasers should check to see if the trustees' powers are specifically limited in any way. If they are not it can be assumed that the trustees have full powers, given to them by the Act.

Further reading

Practice Advice Leaflet No13 'Private Trusts of Land', HM Land Registry

6   Housing Act 1996

Introduction

The Housing Act 1996 is a substantial piece of legislation dealing with many housing-related matters including the social rented sector, houses in multiple occupation, landlord and tenant matters, housing benefit, conduct of tenants, allocation of housing accommodation and homelessness. The conveyancer's interest in the Act is limited to those areas dealing with long leases of houses and flats, including certain changes in the law relating to forfeiture, service charge disputes and insurance disputes. The Act received the Royal Assent on 24 July 1996 and has come into force in phases from September 1996 and throughout 1997 when regulations were passed dealing with the details of the Act.

The law – service charges

Section 81 of the Act restricts the landlord's right to re-enter, or forfeit a lease on the ground of the failure of the tenant to pay a service charge unless the amount of the service charge is agreed or admitted by the tenant or has been the subject of a determination by a court or tribunal. Where the amount of the service charge is subject to determination by the court or tribunal the landlord does not have the right to forfeit the lease for 14 days.

A landlord will now, before exercising a right to forfeit a lease on the ground that the service charge is outstanding, have to issue proceedings for possession or, if the premises have already been vacated, will have to obtain an agreement from the tenant that the amount of the service charge is owing or obtain a Court Order or an Arbitration Award to that effect.

A Service Charge is defined as an amount payable by the tenant of a dwelling as part of or in addition to the rent:

- which is payable, directly or indirectly, for services, repair, maintenance or insurance or the landlord's costs of management; and
- the whole or part of which varies or may vary according to the relevant costs.

The forfeiture changes came into effect on 24 September 1996.

Section 82 of the Act provides that nothing in s81 restricts the right of the landlord to serve a notice under s146(1) Law of Property Act 1925 but that in respect of premises let as a dwelling a notice served on the ground that the tenant has failed to pay a service charge will be ineffective unless it clearly states the tenant's rights under s81 of the Act.

Section 83 deals with the determination of the reasonableness of service charges. Disputes may now be heard by the Leasehold Valuation Tribunal (LVT) and appeals from that tribunal go to the Lands Tribunal. Both the tenant and the landlord can apply for an adjudication to the LVT. The LVT also has the right to determine disputes relating to the insurance of the dwelling. The orders of the LVT are enforceable as if they were county court judgments. The county court still has jurisdiction to deal with service charge disputes but does have a discretion to transfer matters to the LVT; it is likely that tenants will favour the LVT because the procedure is much less formal and there are significant cost advantages. The LVT cannot usually make an order requiring the unsuccessful party to pay the other party's costs.

The purpose of these changes is to balance the powers of landlords against the rights of tenants and there is no doubt that it swings the pendulum considerably in favour of a tenant alleging that the service charge is unreasonable.

Section 83 allows the LVT to determine:

- Whether costs incurred for services, repairs, maintenance, insurance or management are reasonable. The tenant would have to show that the insurance is unsatisfactory in some respect and that the premiums payable are excessive. In the case of *Berrycroft Management Company Limited* v *Sinclair Gardens Investments (Kensington) Limited* (1997) 22 EG 141 CA the tenant was unsuccessful in claiming that the insurance was unreasonable. In that case it was held that a term cannot be implied into the covenants between the management company and the landlord and between the lessees and the management company that the sum charged by the nominated insurer should not be unreasonable, or that a tenant should not be required to pay a substantially higher sum than he could himself arrange with an insurance office of repute. The right of the landlord to nominate the insurance company was in this case unqualified. The fact that the management company could have secured lower rates was irrelevant. However the case was decided in July 1996 before the provisions of the Housing Act 1996 came into force.

- Whether services or works for which costs were incurred are of a reasonable standard.

- Whether an amount payable before costs are incurred is reasonable.

• Whether future costs, if incurred, or future services or works, or a future interim demand will be reasonable.

The service charge changes came into effect on 1 September 1997.

The law – sale of reversion by landlord

The Landlord and Tenant Act 1987 gave certain tenants rights of first refusal where the landlord wishes to dispose of premises where there are two or more flats. Sections 90–94 Housing Act 1996 attempt to address some of the difficulties that have arisen since 1987.

Section 91 resolves the fact that the 1987 Act lacked any adequate enforcement mechanism if the landlord failed to inform the tenants of a sale. It provides that the landlord commits an offence if, without reasonable excuse, he makes a disposal affecting the premises without first giving notice to the qualifying tenants and notifying them of their right of pre-emption. There is a maximum fine of £5,000. The Act also provides that if the landlord is an incorporated body and it is proved that a director, manager or secretary or other similar officer of the company consented or connived in the offence then that person is also guilty of an offence and is liable to be proceeded against and punished accordingly. This part of the Act came into force on 1 October 1996.

Schedule 6 of the Housing Act 1996 provides a strict regime for the landlord's service of the offer, notice on tenants and the subsequent requirements of both the landlord and the tenants. It also sets out in detail the tenants' rights after the landlord has disposed of his interest to a third party. The disposal now includes the exchange of contracts.

Section 93 of the Act requires a new landlord to inform tenants of the assignment, of the landlord's name and address and the fact that the transfer came within the terms of the Act, and that the tenants may have the right to obtain information about the disposal and acquire the landlord's interest. Failure to serve this notice by the next rent date or within a period of two months, whichever is the later, will be a criminal offence punishable by a maximum fine of £2,500. Section 93 came into force on 1 October 1996.

Section 86 allows the tenant to make an application to the LVT for it to appoint a manager when the landlord's management has been poor and there is no other remedy available which would be likely to result in an improvement.

Section 88 allows the compulsory acquisition of a block of flats where the landlord has failed to discharge his obligations relating to repairs, maintenance, insurance or management of the premises, and the appointment of a manager under s85 would not be an adequate remedy or that such a manager has been appointed for two years preceding the date of application. The period was previously three years.

All these provisions have repercussions for the conveyancer. When acting for a purchaser of leasehold property enquiries must be made prior to exchange of contracts to ascertain whether any notices have been received by the seller under the Act. When acting for a landlord the conveyancer must ensure strict adherence to the provisions of the Act.

The law – changes to assured tenancies

Section 96 of the Housing Act 1996 provides that all new assured tenancies will automatically be assured shorthold tenancies. Previously a landlord could only get possession of an assured tenancy by serving a notice seeking possession and obtaining a court order on one of a number of grounds. However, an assured shorthold tenancy allowed the landlord, upon serving the required notice, to get possession automatically as long as the minimum period of six months had expired. There is now no need for a minimum fixed term of six months. It can be a periodic tenancy from the outset.

Section 97 places a duty on the landlord to provide a statement of the terms of the assured shorthold tenancy where these are not otherwise evidenced in writing. These terms are:

- the date on which the tenancy began;
- the rent payable under the tenancy and the dates when the rent is payable;
- any terms allowing for a review of the rent;
- if it is a fixed tenancy, the length of the term.

Failure by the landlord to provide such information within 28 days of a request without a reasonable excuse is a criminal offence punishable by a maximum fine of £2,500.

Although there is now no need for a minimum period of six months any order for possession will not take effect earlier than six months from the beginning of the tenancy.

The law – enfranchisement

The Leasehold Reform Act 1967 gave tenants of houses held on long leases at low rents, who met certain residential qualifications, the right to compulsorily acquire the freehold of their houses or an extension of 50 years on the term of their lease. The Leasehold Reform, Housing and Urban Development Act 1993 gave a right to owners of long leases in blocks of flats the right to collectively acquire the freeholds. These rights depended on payment of low rents and therefore excluded any enfranchisement when a market rent was being paid.

Section 106 and Schedule 9 of the Housing Act 1996 provides that the right to enfranchise is extended to leases that do not comply with the low rents test and that, in respect to houses, are let on a fixed term exceeding 50 years and, to flats, are let on a fixed term exceeding 35 years. The amendment is retrospective to the extent that it will affect leases granted before 1 April 1997.

The right to collective enfranchisement of a block of flats was not available if the freehold of the building was owned by more than one person. This led to freeholders easily being able to avoid the consequences of the 1993 Act. Section 107 of the Housing Act 1996 abolished this restriction. This provision came into force on 1 October 1996.

Further reading

'The Housing Bill – A New Deal For Long Leaseholders', James Driscoll, *Solicitors Journal* 12 July 1996

'Government's Home Rule', Marcia Williams, *Law Society Gazette* 15 January 1997, p18

'Legal Habitat', Michael Tulloch, *Law Society Gazette* 15 January 1997, p20

'Unwitting Criminals', Richard Budge, *Estates Gazette* 15 February 1997

7   Party Wall etc Act 1996

Introduction

The Act extends, with some modifications, the provisions of the London Building Acts (Amendment) Act 1939 to the whole of England and Wales. There has existed in London ever since the Great Fire of 1666 some system of statutory rights for owners over party walls and party structures. The Act enables works to be carried out to party structures and for disputes to be resolved, initially without recourse to the courts. The Act received the Royal Assent on 18 July 1996 and came into force on 1 July 1997.

The law

Section 1 of the Act grants rights to carry out works where there is no existing party structure. If the owner of a building desires to build a party wall or a party fence on the line of a junction, that means on the boundary itself, he is required one month before he intends the building work to start, to serve a notice on the adjoining owner describing what he intends to do. If the adjoining owner consents to the building of a party wall or fence then the new structure can be built on half the land of each of the two owners or in such other position as the two owners agree. The expense of building the wall can be shared in such proportion as has regard to the use made or to be made of the wall by each of the two owners. If the adjoining owner does not give consent within 14 days then the owner building the wall must carry out the work at his own expense and an external wall or fence wall must be placed wholly on his own land.

If the building owner wishes to build a wall wholly on his own land but up to the boundary, he can give notice to the adjoining owner at least one month before he intends to start work, giving a description of the intended wall and the owner will then have the right, after one month but within 12 months, to build footings projecting onto the adjoining owner's land. He must pay the adjoining owner or any adjoining occupier compensation for any damage to the property occasioned by the building of the wall or the placing of the footings or foundations.

There is extensive provision in s2 of the Act that covers work to existing party structures. The building owner has extensive rights, including underpinning, repairing, demolishing and rebuilding and cutting into, including work required to install a damp-proof course and inserting flashing or other weatherproofing. Any damage occasioned by the work must be made good.

Before exercising any rights given to him under s2 a building owner must serve on the adjoining owner a notice giving his personal details, what works he intends to carry out and when. This notice must be served at least two months before the commencement of the work and its effect will cease if the work does not begin with 12 months and is not carried out with due diligence (s3).

The adjoining owner has the right to serve a counter-notice specifying works that need to be carried out for his own convenience, or amendments relating to the proposed works regarding such things as special foundations. The adjoining owner may be responsible for some or all of the costs of these additional works.

If an owner on whom a party structure notice or a counter-notice has been served does not serve a notice indicating his consent to it within 14 days he will be deemed to have dissented to the notice and a dispute will arise.

A building owner who is proposing to excavate or excavate for and erect a building or structure within a specified distance of the adjoining owner's foundations must give one month's notice, with details of the intended works and specifying the depth of the excavations. The adjoining owner can then require that his foundations be underpinned. The defined distances are within three metres of adjoining property where the intended excavation is at a lower level than the foundations of the adjoining owner, or within six metres of the adjoining property where the excavation is so deep that it cuts a line drawn downwards at 45 per cent from the foundations of the adjoining owner.

The Act sets out provisions for compensation in certain circumstances and the right to enter the adjoining land to carry out the work. The Act specifically states it does not authorise any interference with any easements.

Section 10 deals with the resolution of disputes under the Act. The owners can agree on the appointment of one surveyor who can resolve any dispute. If they cannot agree on the appointment of one surveyor then they can each appoint their own surveyor who, in turn, may appoint a third surveyor to adjudicate if the two surveyors cannot agree. The surveyor need not be qualified. Any award made by the surveyor must specify the work which may be carried out and the time and manner of such work. Either party can appeal the decision to the county court but such appeal has to be made within 14 days of the surveyor's award.

Cases

Louis and Another v Sadiq (1997) 16 EG 126 CA (Evans, Henry and Aldous LJJ)

This case was decided under the London Building Acts (Amendment) Act 1939. The appellant, without complying with the procedures under the Act, had started work which interfered with a party wall. After an injunction was granted prohibiting further work, the appellant served the appropriate notice. The appointed surveyor's award was duly made and complied with by the appellants. The Respondents subsequently claimed damages for nuisance, including a claim for mortgage interest, because they could not sell their house. The Appellant would not have been liable at common law if he had followed the procedure under the Act. It was held that the Appellant could not attempt to use the protection that the Act affords from a claim for nuisance during the time that he had not complied with the Act.

Observatory Hill Limited v Camtel Investments (1997) Chancery Division 18 EG 126 Judge Levy QC sitting as a judge of the High Court

There was no right for an adjoining owner who had the benefit of a party wall award to become a person who can enter a caution on the register as a person having an interest in land belonging to the building owner.

Further reading

'Party Walls etc Act 1996', Trevor Aldridge, *Solicitors Journal* 15 November 1996

8   Family Law Act 1996

Introduction

Conveyancers need only concern themselves with ss30–41 and 54–56 of Part IV of the Family Law Act 1996 (FLA). The relevant provisions are included in that part of the FLA dealing with domestic violence. The FLA repeals and replaces, with a few amendments, the Matrimonial Homes Act 1983 (MHA) and came into effect on 1 October 1997.

The law

A right to occupy a matrimonial home under the FLA exists if:

- one spouse is entitled to occupy a dwelling house by virtue of a beneficial estate or interest or contract or any enactment giving that spouse the right to remain in occupation; and
- the other spouse is not so entitled s30(1).

The FLA introduces the term 'matrimonial home rights'. Under the MHA these were called 'rights of occupation'. Matrimonial home rights protect the non-owning spouse's statutory right of occupation of a matrimonial home. It would not be appropriate in a case where husband and wife legally and beneficially jointly own the house. It provides for the non-owning spouse to remain in the home and not be evicted or excluded other than by an order of the court. If the non-owning spouse is not in occupation the Court can allow that spouse to enter and occupy the home s30(2).

The rights extend to where the owning spouse's interest is through a trust. s30(6).

Under s30(7) of the FLA the right can be registered against a future intended matrimonial home.

Matrimonial home rights subsist for the duration of the marriage and therefore terminate on decree absolute or death s30(8). The court has the power under s33(5) to extend these rights beyond divorce or death. The application must be made prior to the termination of the marriage and the court will grant it if it considers it just and reasonable.

A spouse who has an equitable rather than a legal estate interest in the home has the same rights as a spouse who has no interest in the home s30(9).

The Land Registration (Matrimonial Home Rights) Rules 1997 provide for registration of matrimonial home rights. If the home is unregistered land the rights should be registered as a Class F, using Form K2. If the home is registered land the rights should be registered at the Land Registry using Form MH1. The registration constitutes a charge on the matrimonial home.

If a contract for sale of the matrimonial home provides for vacant possession upon completion, there is an implied term that the seller will procure cancellation of the registered matrimonial rights prior to completion, Para 3 Schedule 4.

If the rights are not registered then they cannot be enforced against anybody who acquires an interest in the matrimonial home.

Conveyancers must never give an undertaking to discharge matrimonial home rights on completion of a sale unless they have the application to cancel the notice of a matrimonial home right (Form MH4 for registered land and Form K13 unregistered land) signed by the registering spouse. Conveyancers are not allowed to sign cancellation forms on behalf of their clients.

The occupying spouse can only protect any matrimonial home rights in respect of one house at any one time. If there are two matrimonial homes and the occupying spouse lives in one and wishes to move to the other a fresh application, in Form MH1 or, K2, must be made. The forms require disclosure as to whether or not there is any previous protection, and such previous protection is then cancelled, Para 2 Schedule 4.

Sections 33 to 36 of the FLA provide that associated persons, and that includes cohabitees, can apply for occupation orders against the other cohabitee. These do not, however, confer any matrimonial home rights which could be enforced against third parties. This is designed to provide a short-term remedy in cases where there may be domestic violence or an urgent housing need.

Sections 54–56 deal with the effect on mortgages of matrimonial home rights. Any right of possession of a mortgagee is disregarded when determining whether a spouse is entitled to occupy a dwelling house. A spouse however has no greater rights against a mortgagee to occupy the house than the person with an estate or interest.

Further reading

Land Registry Explanatory Reading 4, 'Protecting Matrimonial Home Rights under the Family Law Act 1996'.

Land Registry Practice Leaflet 10, 'Applications under the Family Law Act 1996 Affecting Registered Land'.

9   Land Registration Act 1997

Introduction

This very important piece of legislation came into effect on 1st April 1998. It has important consequences for the conveyancer and extends the range of events which lead to compulsory first registration of title, in an effort to accelerate the process of Land Registration throughout the country.

The law

It is now compulsory to register a property after any of the following dispositions of unregistered land:

- the conveyance of a freehold estate;
- a lease for a term of years absolute of more than 21 years;
- an assignment of a term of years absolute which on the date of the assignment has more than 21 years to run;
- an assent including a vesting assent which is a disposition of the freehold estate or a term of years absolute on which the date of the disposition has more than 21 years to run;
- the disposition of unregistered land which is a legal mortgage of the freehold estate or a term of years absolute which on the date of the mortgage has more than 21 years to run as long as when the mortgage was created it took effect as a mortgage to be protected by the deposit of documents relating to the estate or the term of years and at the time it comes to be registered it is a first mortgage.

The Act gives the Lord Chancellor power to extend further dispositions which must be registered.

The Act very helpfully lists all the transactions which require registration. These are as follows:

- Conveyance on Sale
- Exchange with equality money
- Conveyance in return for the allotment or transfer of shares in a Company
- Conveyance in consideration of a rent charge or annuity
- Compulsory purchase by Deed Poll

- Compulsory acquisition of a secure tenancy under the Housing Act 1985
- A purchase under Part IV Housing Act 1988
- Surrender of a lease for money consideration which does not result in an immediate merger
- An assignment on sale of leasehold land held for a term of years absolute having more than 21 years to run from date of delivery of the assignment
- A grant of a term of years absolute of not more than 21 years from the date of delivery of the grant
- Gift of a freehold or leasehold interest with more than 21 years to run
- Voluntary settlement involving a freehold or a leasehold interest with more than 21 years to run
- First mortgage secured by deposit of Title Deeds involving a freehold or leasehold interest with more than 21 years to run
- Assent of a freehold or leasehold interest with more than 21 years to run
- A vesting assent of a freehold or leasehold interest with more than 21 year to run
- Exchange with no equality money of a freehold or a leasehold interest with more than 21 years to run
- An agreement to extinguish an existing debt if land is transferred involving a freehold or a leasehold interest with more than 21 years to run
- A conveyance in pursuance of an Order of the Court involving a freehold or leasehold interest with more than 21 years to run.

Land Registry changes

The Land Registry has used the introduction of the Act to effect a number of changes to their forms. The old forms were accepted by the Land Registry up to 30 October 1998, after which date the Land Registry has indicated that under no circumstances will the old forms be acceptable.

Details of New Forms

New Form	Use of Form	Old Form
AP1	Application for registration of dealing of whole	A4
AS1	Assent or appropriation of whole	56
AS2	Assent or appropriation of registered charge	
CS	Continuation sheet	
CT1	Application for caution against first registration with statutory declaration	13/14
DL	List of documents	A13
DS1	Discharge of registered charge	53,53(Co)
DS2	Application form for use when DS1 is the only instrument being registered	
FR1	Application form for first registration	1A, 1B, 1F, 1K, 2A, 2B, 3A, 3B
TR1	Transfer of whole	19, 19(JP), 19(Co), 32, 33, 44
TR2	Transfer of whole under a power of sale	31
TR3	Transfer of registered charge	54
TR4	Transfer of a portfolio of registered charges	

Further reading

'Survival Pack', HM Land Registry

'Land Registration Act 1997', *Law Society Gazette* 23 April 1997, p30

10 Negligence in Conveyancing

Introduction

The efforts made by the Conservative government from 1979 onwards to extend owner-occupation throughout the United Kingdom has created a huge mortgage lending industry. The unsophisticated mutual societies, often run on a part-time basis by accountants and solicitors, had become huge national, and in some cases international, banks. With their financial growth their power and influence has also mushroomed. In the mid-1980s it appeared that lending money on the security of residential property was a one-way ticket to success. As long as the lending was less than the value of the property what could possibly go wrong? The values of properties in the mid-1980s were rising at 20 per cent or 30 per cent per year. In some years and in some areas the rises would be even higher. The lenders became very complacent and even though they were becoming very sophisticated and well-organised by the mid-1980s they did not see the property recession coming. Many lenders had extremely poor lending policies in the mid-to-late 1980s. Some lenders made no enquiries whatsoever about the financial status of their borrowers. Those who specialised in re-mortgages were inclined not to take a reference from an existing lender in case the existing lender persuaded the borrower to stay with them. In August 1988 the dual-mortgage tax relief was abolished. The substantial increases in the prices of properties in the late-1980s could not be sustained. The economy went into recession and property prices followed. Extensive negative equity was a phenomenon that was to last for some ten years. The poor lending policies of some organisations would never have been exposed if prices of properties had continued to rise. Lenders suddenly found that many of their borrowers had lost their jobs and could not afford the repayments. They took possession proceedings and found that when they came to sell as mortgagees in possession they obtained prices substantially less than the outstanding mortgages. They looked around to see from whom they could recover these losses. Then began a period of nearly ten years in which the solicitor's profession was to be asked to pick up the cost of the lenders' losses.

There is no doubt that the quality of some conveyancing carried out in the late-1980s was poor. The volume of conveyancing was substantial and staff with too little experience or training were often expected to handle intricate transactions and this greatly contributed to the losses the profession has had to bear over the last eight or nine years. In the Solicitors Indemnity Fund's third annual report, for the year ending 1 August 1990, there was no mention of any problem in relation to conveyancing claims. In fact, at that time the report did not even refer to claims made in relation to conveyancing matters. In the tenth annual report for the year ending 31 August 1997, a substantial part related to conveyancing and lender-related claims. In the year ending 31 August 1997, 42 per cent of claims by value related to residential conveyancing, 11 per cent to commercial conveyancing and 12 per cent to property and mortgage matters. Conveyancing therefore made up a 64 per cent of claims by value on the Indemnity Fund.

Mortgage Express Limited v *Bowerman & Partners* [1996] 2 All ER 836 Court of Appeal (Sir Thomas Bingham MR, Millett and Schiemann LJJ)

Facts
The defendant firm of solicitors acted for both the borrower and the lender on the purchase of a property for £220,000. The solicitors discovered during the course of the conveyancing transaction that the property had recently been sold for £150,000. The solicitors notified the borrower but did not tell the lender.

Held
The solicitors' duty went beyond title and even beyond the specific matters referred to in the solicitor's instructions. Sir Thomas Bingham MR said:

'If in the course of investigating title, a solicitor discovers facts that a reasonably competent solicitor would realise might have a bearing on the valuation of a lender's security or some other ingredient of the lending decision then it is his duty to point this out.'

Sir Thomas Bingham went on to say that on the facts in this case if the conveyancer had applied his mind to the facts he would have come to the conclusion that the valuation might be suspect and should have then reported the matter to the lender. It was worrying for conveyancers that such a responsibility should be placed on their shoulders. It is difficult enough to deal with the mechanics of a conveyancing transaction without having the responsibility of checking the lenders' valuation report.

There is no doubt that some conveyancers had difficulty in the late-1980s in accepting that the lender client was of equal importance as the borrower client. There must, however, be doubt that conveyancers could ever had appreciated that they had the responsibilities to report information to the lender which might or might not affect their decision to lend. *Mortgage Express* was the high-water mark of the liability for a solicitor to report information to the lender.

National Home Loans Corp Plc v Giffen Couch & Archer (A Firm) [1997] 3 All ER 808 Court of Appeal (Leggatt, Peter Gibson and Hobhouse LJJ)

Facts

The plaintiff was a centralised lender operating from a single location and was dependent on the introduction of clients by intermediaries. Part of its business came from re-mortgage transactions and the mortgage in this case was provided under a self-certification scheme whereby, upon a re-mortgage, intending borrowers of sums of up to £100,000, which did not exceed 75 per cent of the valuation of the property, could themselves certify their incomes and their good conduct as mortgagors, and a reference from the existing lenders was not required. It had been accepted by the plaintiff in evidence that borrowers in financial difficulties under an existing mortgage seeking a re-mortgage, would stand a greater chance of success on applying to the plaintiff than if they had applied to a lender who required independent verification of the information supplied by the intending borrowers.

The defendants, a firm of solicitors, acted for both the lender and the borrower. The defendants were sent details of the mortgage offer but were not told whether it was to be a status (where the lender confirms the borrower's earnings) or non-status mortgage. The defendants were also sent a standard printed form of instructions to solicitors and licensed conveyancers. The defendants were instructed to investigate the title to the property and to advise if any condition of the offer of the loan, or any condition of the instructions, had not been or could not be complied with. They were also instructed to report on title on a standard form. The defendants were required to certify amongst other things that they were not aware of any material change in the borrower's circumstances subsequent to the date of the offer of the loan. There was no requirement to report on the state of account of any existing mortgage and the solicitors were not given a copy of the application form completed by the borrower. There were, in fact, inaccuracies in the mortgage application form completed by the borrower, and by the time the matter was about to be completed the defendant solicitors were aware that there were arrears of over £4,000 on the mortgage with the previous mortgagee. The defendant solicitors did not pass that information on to the lender. The matter was completed and the borrower quickly fell into arrears. The property was eventually sold and the lender sought to recover its loss from the solicitors.

First Instance
It was held that the defendants were under a duty to tell the lender about the arrears on the previous mortgage.

Court of Appeal
The Court of Appeal reversed that decision. Gibson LJ said:

'The factors which seem to me to be relevant to determining the extent of the defendant's duty in the present case are these:

1) The instructions from the plaintiff required the defendants to act for the plaintiff "in the preparation of a mortgage ... in accordance with the Notes for Guidance and the documents provided..." Any solicitor of ordinary competence and experience would realise that the defendants primary function was to make sure that the plaintiff received a valid and effective first mortgage on the property, and that required in particular that the plaintiff should receive a good and marketable title. The approval of the title by the defendants was an express condition of the loan.

2) The plaintiff, an experienced commercial lender, provided its own detailed printed instructions to solicitors. Those instructions specified the particular matters on which the plaintiff required to be advised. This made clear, for example, that the investigation of title should go beyond ordinary conveyancing matters, but extended to matters which might the affect valuation put upon the property ... they were required to advise if any information suggested that the property was not to be the principal residence of Mr and Mrs Choudhry for the sole continuing occupation of them and their family. The plaintiff provided its own form of report on title which stated precisely what the solicitor was required to certify. In these circumstances, ... there is limited room here for treating the scope of the duty of care as extending to require the solicitor to take action which has not been expressly required by the plaintiff in its instructions.

3) Subject to para 6 of the report on title, the only action which the defendants were instructed to take relating to financial circumstances of Mr and Mrs Choudhry was twofold: to do a bankruptcy search and to report on any matter revealed by the search.

4) The plaintiff did not send a copy of the application by Mr and Mrs Choudhry to the defendants and there was no evidence that they knew of any of its contents.

5) Further, the report on title, in requiring the defendants to certify that they were not aware of any material change in the circumstances of Mr and Mrs Choudhry subsequent to the date of the offer of the loan, would

45

naturally lead the defendants to believe that, subject only to a clear bankruptcy search being obtained, the plaintiff was satisfied that the circumstances of Mr and Mrs Choudhry at that date was such that they were appropriate borrowers. The defendants did not know what enquiries, if any, had been made by the plaintiff. Mrs Butler, a Legal Executive who was employed by the defendants and who ... dealt with the matter, presumed that the plaintiff would have sought a reference from Western Trust.

Mortgage Express v *Bowerman* was distinguished on its facts.

This is an extremely important decision in favour of the conveyancer. Many other cases commenced by lenders depended upon its outcome. A conveyancer is not under a duty to report information to the lender unless his instructions require him to do so. It is important, however, to sound a note of caution in that in recent years lenders have tightened up their specific instructions to solicitors and those instructions are now more likely to place a contractual obligation on the conveyancer to divulge any information which they come across which might affect the decision by the lenders to make the initial mortgage offer. There is no doubt, however, that the decision in *Giffen Couch & Archer* has saved the Solicitors Indemnity Fund many millions of pounds in claims. The conveyancing profession will be relieved that the apparent unstoppable onslaught by lenders has come to an end. *Giffen Couch & Archer* represents a significant reversal for lenders and brings the law more closely into line with what conveyancers believed their responsibilities to be in the late 1980s and early 1990s.

Birmingham Mid-Shires Mortgage Services Limited (formerly Hypo-Mortgage Services Ltd) and Another v David Parry & Co (A Firm) and Another [1997] EGCS 150 Court of Appeal (Staughton, Eward and Mummery LJJ)

Facts
This was another case where the plaintiffs were centralised lenders and agreed to lend £487,500 secured on a property called The Mill. The borrower informed the plaintiffs that the defendant firm of solicitors would act for the borrower and the plaintiffs instructed the firm also to act for them. In the application form that the borrower had submitted to the plaintiffs he had given details of an existing mortgage and an unsecured charge on The Mill. Condition 8 of the plaintiffs' General Conditions provided: 'The applicant's existing mortgage(s), if any, must be redeemed on or before completion of this advance'; and Special Condition 14 of the

Special Conditions of the mortgage offer was in virtually identical terms. The borrower made no payments under the mortgage and the plaintiffs obtained possession. They ultimately sold The Mill for £240,000 and then proceeded to claim the difference between the mortgage advance and the net sum received on the sale in an action for breach of duty against the defendant firm of solicitors. They complained, inter alia, that the defendants should have informed them that B would be unable, on completion of the advance, to pay off loans secured on two other properties in Wales.

Held

On the true construction of General Condition 8 and Special Condition 14 the borrower was not obliged to inform the plaintiffs of the existence of the mortgages on properties other than The Mill and a reasonable, competent solicitor would not have informed the plaintiffs about mortgages over other properties which B was not obliged by the conditions to redeem. The defendants' principal duty to the plaintiffs was to investigate and report on matters of title to the property to be charged and to ensure that they obtained a valid first charge on that property. The defendant firm of solicitors was accordingly not in breach of its duty to the plaintiffs.

Comment

The Court of Appeal have confirmed their approach in *Giffen Couch & Archer*. The lenders in this case were trying to further extend the boundaries of conveyancers' liability by suggesting that they should be informed of mortgages on other properties not the subject of the lenders' charge because it might be relevant as to the ability of the borrower to discharge his responsibilities under their mortgage.

Breach of Trust

Target Holdings Limited v Redferns (A Firm) and Another [1996] I AC 421 House of Lords (Lords Keith of Kinkel, Ackner, Jauncey of Tullichettle, Browne-Wilkinson and Lloyd of Berwick)

Facts

A company agreed to buy two properties. The estimated value and purchase price of the properties was stated to be £2,000,000 having been valued, allegedly negligently, by a firm of estate agents. In fact, the properties were originally bought for £775,000 by another company owned by the same individuals and sold for £1,250,000 to yet another company owned by the same individuals, who then sold them on to the eventual purchaser for £2,000,000. In that way the purchase price had been uplifted from the original £775,000 to £2,000,000. The plaintiffs approved the loan of £1,525,000 and made a mortgage offer of that amount to the purchaser. The plaintiffs also instructed the defendant solicitors to act for them and prior to completion paid the solicitors the mortgage advance. The solicitors passed the money down the chain to the other two companies who used the money to purchase the property for £775,000. The defendant solicitors notified the plaintiffs that the charge had been completed, although at that time the transaction had not in fact taken place. The balance of the loan advanced by the plaintiffs was with the knowledge of the solicitors retained by one of the intermediary companies. The plaintiffs subsequently repossessed the properties and sold them for £500,000. The plaintiffs brought an action against the defendants for breach of trust. In proceedings for summary judgment, the defendants accepted that they had received the loan moneys from the plaintiffs, as agents for the plaintiffs and until authorised by the plaintiffs to release the moneys they held them in trust for the plaintiffs, and that they had committed a breach of trust when they transferred the moneys before the contract for the purchase of the properties and the mortgage had been completed. However, the defendants claimed that the breach of trust was technical only and that the plaintiffs had not suffered any loss because the defendants had signed the mortgages to which the plaintiffs were entitled, albeit at a later date.

Held

By a majority decision, the Court of Appeal held that the obligation of a trustee who had committed a breach of trust was to put the trust fund in the same position as it would have been if no breach had taken place, and where the breach consisted in the wrongful paying away of trust moneys to a stranger so that there was an immediate loss it was not necessary that there should be an enquiry as to whether the loss would have happened if there had been no breach, since there was an obvious casual connection. The remedy was compensation in the form of restitution of the trust fund. There was no question of causation and no consideration was given as to what would have happened had the trustee performed his obligations.

The House of Lords reversed the decision of the Court of Appeal and decided that a trustee who committed a breach of trust was not liable to compensate the beneficiary for losses which the beneficiary would in any event have suffered if there had been no breach.

Comment

Since this case, lenders have commonly incorporated an allegation of breach of trust in their claims against conveyancers in their efforts to side-step issues of contributory negligence and losses due to the drop in the property market.

Bristol & West Building Society v *Mothew* [1996] 4 All ER 698

The Court of Appeal suggested that a breach of trust of fiduciary duty must entail some disloyalty or infidelity. Mere incompetence was not sufficient for the lenders to succeed.

Facts

The solicitor had inadvertently failed to tell the lender that there was a second charge on the property which he was specifically required to do in his instructions. The solicitor admitted negligence but argued that if he had informed the lender of the existence and amount of the second charge it would not have made any difference to the lender's decision to proceed with the mortgage. The solicitor also argued that any loss suffered by the lender was not attributable to his negligence. The lender had lost because the value of the property had fallen in the market. The Court of Appeal rejected it on the basis that it had simply been the solicitor's incompetence that had caused the loss and there had been no element of fraud.

Comment

The message coming from these cases appears that if a conveyancer knowingly misleads the lender he may be required to repay the trust money in full. If he is just innocently misleading, or misrepresenting the position, he is still negligent and may well be in breach of contract, but the lender must demonstrate that he would not have continued with the loan if the breach had not occurred.

Breach of Warranty of Authority

Penn v *Bristol & West Building Society and Others* [1997] 3 All ER 470 Court of Appeal (Staughton, Waite and Waller LJJ)

Facts

Mr and Mrs Penn owned their matrimonial home in joint names with a mortgage in favour of the Bradford & Bingley Building Society. Mr Penn and his business partner Mr Moore were in financial difficulties and devised a scheme whereby Mr Wilson would pose as a purchaser buying the matrimonial home for £80,000 with mortgage funding of £75,000 from the Bristol & West Building Society. The money generated from the mortgage would discharge Mr Moore and Mr Penn's indebtedness. Mrs Penn had no knowledge of the planned sale. The solicitors handling the sale never confirmed instructions with her but purported to act on behalf of both her and Mr Penn on his instructions alone. The contract and transfer signatures of Mrs Penn were forged by Mr Penn. The solicitors discharged the Penns' mortgage and paid the balance to Mr Penn's bank. Mr Penn used the funds for his own purposes without Mrs Penn's knowledge or consent. The fraud was discovered and the Bristol & West Building Society could not register their charge because no title passed to Mr Wilson.

Held

The Court of Appeal confirmed that the solicitors had acted negligently in failing to ascertain that they had Mrs Penn's instructions and were also liable for breach of warranty of authority because they had held themselves out as having authority for the joint owners in the sale. The solicitors were therefore liable to the Bristol & West Building Society.

> 'Where a person by word or conduct represents that he has authority to act on behalf of another, and a third party is induced by such representation to act in a manner which he would not have acted if that representation had not been made, the first mentioned person is deemed to warrant the representation is true, and is liable for any loss caused to such third party by breach of implied warranty, even if he acted in good faith in a mistaken belief that he had such authority.'

Comment

The worrying aspect of this case is that the solicitors would have been liable even if they had been misled by someone who had been posing as Mrs Penn. Conveyancers therefore have an obligation to check identities even if such obligation is not contained in the lender's instructions. Conveyancers must be very careful about signing contracts on behalf of their clients' as this might amount to a warranty.

Barclays Bank plc v Weeks Legg & Dean; Barclays Bank plc v Layton Lougher & Company; Barclays Bank plc v NE Hopkin John & Company and Others [1998] 3 WLR 213 Court of Appeal (Millett, Pill and May LJJ)

Facts

This case before the Court of Appeal concerns the proper construction of a standard form of undertaking given to Barclays Bank Plc by solicitors to facilitate the provision of funds to buy land. The undertaking was in a form agreed between the Law Society and the banks and reads as follows:

UNDERTAKING TO SOLICITOR

To send deeds/land certificate to bank on completion of a purchase, the bank and/or the customer having provided the purchase moneys.

To Barclays Bank Plc

If you provide facilities to my/our client ... for the purchase of the freehold/leasehold property ...

I/We undertake:

A. That all sums received from you or your customer for the purpose of this transaction will be applied solely for acquiring a good marketable title to such property and in paying any necessary deposit, legal costs and disbursements in connection with such purpose. The purchase price contemplated is £   gross and with apportionments and any necessary disbursements is not expected to exceed £   .

B. After the property has been acquired by   and all necessary stamping and registration completed to send the title deeds and/or land certificate and documents to you and in the meantime to hold them to your order.

In each of the cases to which these Appeals relate, the Bank brought an action against solicitors who gave the above undertaking for damages for breach of the undertaking. In each case, the Bank claimed that the solicitor parted with money on completion of the purchase of the property but failed to obtain a title to the property which provided satisfactory security for the Bank. In the first action, this was because the property was subject to a right of way which precluded its successful development. In the second action, it was because there was no access to the property and there were insufficient rights to drainage and other services to allow for its development. In the third action, the property was owned by three co-owners. One of them had not consented to the sale and her signature on the conveyance of sale was forged. In the first action, at first instance, the Bank failed. In the second action, the Bank succeeded and, in the third action, the Bank failed. In each of the actions at first instance, the Judges adopted different approaches to the effect of the undertaking.

All three cases had certain common features:

1. In each case the Bank was lending money to its own customer for a particular transaction known to the Bank.

2. The transaction was briefly described in the undertaking.

3. The extent of the Bank's knowledge of the transaction was not known to the solicitors.

4. Except in the second action and then only in relation to the registration of its security, the Bank did not instruct the solicitors to act for it in the transaction.

5. The Bank did not ask the solicitors to provide a report on title or to advise in relation to any aspect of the transaction.

6. The solicitors were not paid by the Bank for their services.

7. The obligation undertaken by the solicitor is not to part with the money except in the circumstances prescribed. The function of the undertaking was to prescribe the terms upon which the solicitor received the money remitted by the Bank. The money belongs to the Bank and the solicitor is authorised to disperse it in accordance with the terms of the undertaking but not otherwise. If the solicitor parts with the money otherwise and in accordance with the undertaking it is a breach of a contractual undertaking and a breach of trust.

Decision

Solicitors give these types of undertaking every day of the week and it is perhaps surprising that the Court of Appeal has not dealt with these issues before. Millett LJ, in his judgment, set out three issues that were raised:

1. The meaning to be attributed to the expression 'for acquiring a good marketable title to such property'.

2. Whether the obligation which the solicitors assumed by giving the undertaking is an absolute or a qualified obligation.

3. Whether any of the solicitors undertook a duty to advise the Bank either generally in relation to the transaction in question or in relation to the vendor's title.

A good marketable title

The banks admitted that this meant a freehold title free from incumbrances. They suggested that this meant that it was better than a good title since is must be both good in the sense of being without blemish and marketable in the sense that it related to the saleability of the property. Millett LJ did not agree. The wording of the undertaking related just to the title itself and the inclusion of the word marketable did not relate to the saleability of the property but related to the quality of the title. Some titles are not perfect and, while it would be acceptable to a keen purchaser, it might not be acceptable to a reluctant purchaser. The Bank suggested that if the property was being acquired subject to a right of way or other incumbrance, the solicitor should have stated that in the description of the property in the undertaking itself. Millett LJ disagreed. The undertaking simply contains a brief description of the property to identify the transaction to which the undertaking relates, not the property the purchaser was acquiring.

The effect of the undertaking

Millett LJ said that the undertaking was to be construed as an undertaking not to part with the money except for a good marketable title to the property which is the subject matter of the transaction briefly described in the document (ie the undertaking). The solicitor is, in effect, giving an assurance to the bank that, in return for its money, it would obtain the security which it expects. The value of the security depends on the nature and extent of the property which is acquired, the value of the property and the bank's ability to realise its security by sale if necessary.

Absolute or qualified obligation

Are the solicitors liable if they part with the money without, in fact, obtaining a good marketable title to the property, even though this is through no fault of their own; or are they only liable if such failure is the result of their own default? Millett LJ decided that it must be construed on the basis of what a reasonably competent solicitor acting with proper skill and care would accept as a good marketable title. In his judgment he gives his reasons as follows:

1. It would be inconceivable that the parties would expect their solicitor to assume a more onerous obligation to a bank, which was not his client and is not being charged for his services, than he assumed towards his own client.

2. The undertaking related to the investigation of the vendor's title in addition to the due execution of the conveyance by the vendor. It would be impossible for a purchaser's solicitor to give an unqualified guarantee of the vendor's title.

3. The purchaser's solicitors could have taken reasonable precautions to ensure that the legal charge was properly executed by his own client but, for instance, he depended on the vendor's solicitors to ensure that the conveyance was properly executed by the vendor.

4. Given that the purpose of the undertaking is to prescribe the terms on which the solicitor is authorised to part with trust money which belongs in equity to the bank, it is difficult to see why he should assume a more onerous obligation in contract than he assumes by virtue of the trust.

Millett LJ, therefore, found that the undertaking should be construed as subjecting the solicitor to qualified obligations only. This would bring his obligations governed by the undertaking into conformity with his obligations to his own client, as well as with his trust obligations to the bank and will not involve exposing him to a liability which no solicitor could be properly advised to accept.

The Court of Appeal decided that, in the first and third case, the appeals would be dismissed and the solicitors were not liable. In the second case, the Court agreed with the judge at first instance that the solicitor did not investigate the title with proper skill and care and he was, therefore, in breach of his qualified undertaking and that liability had been established.

Pill LJ in his concurring judgment said:

> 'I regard it as inconceivable that a document for general use which has obvious and sensible purposes in a property transaction can have been intended by the parties to provide the Bank with a guarantee as to title and put the solicitor in the position of the Banks' insurer for the purposes of title. ...'

This case follows a series of cases where lenders have endeavoured to recover from solicitors when their borrowers have defaulted. The pendulum appears to be swinging back in favour of solicitors away from the lenders and this case follows the Court of Appeal's decision in *Giffen Couch & Archer* in clearly defining solicitors' liability to lenders.

What conveyancers can to avoid claims

Conveyancers should be very careful about sending their files to lenders. Some lenders automatically ask for a file if they have repossessed and there is a shortfall. They often fail to disclose to the conveyancer the real reason for wanting the file. The file is then scrutinised by the lender's solicitors who try and find some sort of breach of duty with which to claim against the conveyancer to make up the shortfall.

Nationwide Building Society v *Various Solicitors* (1998) The Times 5 February (Mr Justice Blackburne)

This is authority for what documents a conveyancer can disclose to a lender client, where there exists at the same time a separate retainer with a borrower. It decided which documents a conveyancer can retain and which he has to send to the lender. Documents where privilege attaches to the borrower must not be disclosed to the lender. Each document has to be considered separately and if it was created for the purpose of giving or obtaining legal advice for the borrower it is privileged and need not be disclosed to the lender. If there is any doubt then privilege should be claimed. Where documents have been created as part of the retainer for the lender then they must be disclosed. A lender may try and obtain the borrower's consent to waive the privilege and then if successful the whole file has to be disclosed.

Documents that are privileged
- Correspondence between borrower and conveyancer
- Attendance notes of meetings and telephone calls between borrower and conveyancer
- Completion statement
- Invoice to borrower

Documents that must be disclosed
- Correspondence between conveyancer and lender
- Mortgage offer
- Copy report on title
- Client ledger
- Pre-contract searches and enquiries and replies
- Requisitions on title and answers
- Abstracts, epitomes and office copy entries
- Contracts, transfers and conveyances

Further reading

'Tell The Lender If Loan Will Go Bad', Caroline Shea & Anthony Tanny, *Property Week*, 31 January 1997

'Conveyancing: Warranty of Authority', Simon Pizzey, *Solicitors Journal*, 30 May 1997

'Solicitor's Duty to Lenders', Wanda Barry, *Law Society Gazette*, 2 July 1997, p31

'Put On The Spot', Anthony Judge, *Estates Gazette*, 19 July 1997

'Breach of duty – Lenders', David Turner and Gary Oldroyd, *Law Society Gazette*, 30 July 1997, p31

'Professional Negligence', *Solicitors Journal Update,* 31 October 1997

'Privileged Access', David Turn at Gary Oldroyd, *Law Society Gazette*, 7 May 1998, p36

SIF Fact Sheet Conveyancing 1 – Claims Preventions For Conveyancers

11 Solicitors
Borrower)
1998

The Council of the Law Society a̶
Rules 1990 on 24 September 199̶
(Lender and Borrower) Amendme̶
come into force on 1 June 1999. T̶
conveyancers to lenders.

Until the 1960s, lenders instructed the̶
to a borrower. The Halifax Building
instructing the borrowers' solicitors to a̶ ...̶ was felt
that, on balance, a solicitor could act f̶ ...̶ and borrower –
conflict was unlikely to arise as the lende̶ ...̶ructions were generally
confined to ensuring good title. The lenders have widened the ambit of
their instructions to buyers' solicitors so that today there is far more
likelihood that conflicts of interest will arise. This has lead to a substantial
increase in claims by lenders against solicitors and, in turn, substantial
pressure on the Solicitors Indemnity Fund. The lenders have endeavoured
to increase solicitors' responsibilities to areas in which the solicitors have
no knowledge or experience. Solicitors were becoming liable on matters of
valuation and on whether the borrower had the resources to maintain their
payments under the mortgage. Non-status mortgages meant that lenders
carried out little investigation as to the borrower's ability to repay the
mortgage. The lenders tried to protect themselves by passing on liabilities
and responsibilities to their solicitor, and when they lost money they
sought to recover the loss from the solicitors.

There is no way that individual solicitors can limit their liability. Lenders
send out their instructions with standard form documentation and there is
quite clearly an inequality of bargaining power. When problems become
apparent, the parties are often anxious to exchange contracts or complete
and there is pressure on the solicitor to proceed despite the problems that
he has discovered.

In 1994 the Law Society issued a Report on the future of conveyancing
called 'Adapting for the Future'. It suggested amending Practice Rule 6 to
require separate representation of lender and borrower. The proposal did
not meet with approval from the profession or, indeed, the lenders. The
Society then entered into negotiations with a group of lenders to try to

...structions'. Those negotiations have been
.. Whenever there was a judicial decision that
lenders, they endeavoured to amend the Standard
is to negate that decision.

at has eventually been agreed by the Council of the Law
o define by practice rule the scope of instructions that may be
d when a solicitor acts for both lender and borrower. The rule
nes the scope of a solicitor's retainer with a lender in all transactions
where the solicitor is also acting for the borrower, but also requires the use
of a standard certificate of title in residential transactions. Joint
representation of lender and borrower will, therefore, continue but the
new rule prohibits solicitors from accepting instructions which are
unacceptably wide from lenders when they are also acting for the
borrower. The rule, with amendments taking effect from 1 June 1999, will
substantially reduce the risk of conflict of interest and hopefully reduce
further claims on the Indemnity Fund.

The rule provides for lenders to self-certify that their instructions comply
with Rule 6. The Law Society will be publishing a list of lenders that have
indicated they intend to comply with the new rule. If the lenders
instructions do not confirm that they comply with Rule 6 then there is an
obligation on the solicitor to write to the lender to make it clear that the
solicitor can only continue to act for the lender on the limited basis of
Rule 6.

Solicitors acting for lender and borrower in a residential mortgage

The lenders instructions must not extend beyond the limitations set out in
paragraphs 3(c) and 3(e) of the new rule. Those limitations are designed to
ensure that a solicitor does not act for the lender on matters which the
solicitor is not qualified to deal with.

The solicitor must use a certificate of title required by paragraph 3(d) of
the new rule.

The solicitor cannot act if the lender insists on its own report on title or
asks in its instructions for confirmation of matters beyond those contained
in paragraphs 3(c) and 3(e).

Solicitors acting for lender and borrower in a commercial transaction

The lenders instructions must not extend beyond the limitations set out in paragraph 3(c) and 3(e) of the new rule but there is no requirement to use the prescribed certificate of title. However solicitors will not be able to complete the lender's certificate of title if it deals with matters beyond those set out in paragraph 3(c) and 3(e).

The new rule has significant repercussions for conveyancers and is set out below in full.

Note: The changes to Practice Rule 6(3) – Solicitors' Practice Rules 1990 and the notes are shown in bold type

Solicitors' Practice (Lender and Borrower) Amendment Rule 1998

Rule dated 29 September 1998 made by the Council of the Law Society with the concurrence of the Master of the Rolls under section 31 of the Solicitors Act 1974 and section 9 of the Administration of Justice Act 1985

(1) In Rule 6 of the Solicitors' Practice Rules 1990 (avoiding conflicts of interest in conveyancing, property selling and mortgage related services) as amended on 16 January 1998 by the Solicitors' Practice (Property Selling) Amendment Rule 1998, delete paragraph (3) and substitute:

'(3) (Solicitor acting for lender and borrower)

(a) A solicitor must not act for both lender and borrower on the grant of a mortgage of land:

(i) if a conflict of interest exists or arises;

(ii) on the grant of a private mortgage of land at arm's length;

(iii) if, in the case of an institutional mortgage of property to be used as a private residence only, the lender's mortgage instructions extend beyond the limitations contained in paragraphs (3)(c) and (3)(e), or do not permit the use of the certificate of title required by paragraph (3)(d); or

(iv) if, in the case of any other institutional mortgage, the lender's mortgage instructions extend beyond the limitations contained in paragraphs (3)(c) and (3)(e).

(b) A solicitor who proposes to act for both lender and borrower on the grant of an institutional mortgage of land, must first inform the lender in writing of the circumstances if:

(i) the solicitor or a member of his or her immediate family is a borrower; or

(ii) the solicitor proposes to act for seller, buyer, and lender in the same transaction.

(c) A solicitor acting for both lender and borrower in an institutional mortgage may only accept or act upon instructions from the lender which are limited to the following matters:

(i) taking reasonable steps to check the borrower's identity against a photograph and/or specimen signature supplied by the lender;

(ii) making appropriate searches relating to the property in public registers (for example, local searches, commons registration searches), and reporting any results specified by the lender or which the solicitor considers may adversely affect the lender;

(iii) making enquiries on legal matters relating to the property reasonably specified by the lender, and reporting the replies;

(iv) reporting on how the borrower says that the purchase money (other than the mortgage advance) is to be provided;

(v) reporting if the seller has not owned or been the registered owner of the property for at least six months;

(vi) confirming that the buildings insurance is in place for the sum required by the lender;

(vii) investigating title to the property and rights enjoyed by occupiers of it, reporting any defects revealed, advising on the need for any consequential statutory declarations or indemnity insurance, and effecting indemnity cover if required by the lender;

(viii) reporting on any financial charges secured on the property which will continue to affect the property after completion of the mortgage;

(ix) in the case of a leasehold property, confirming that the lease contains the terms stipulated by the lender and does not include any terms specified by the lender as unacceptable;

(x) making appropriate pre-completion searches, including a bankruptcy search against the borrower and any guarantor;

(xi) receiving, releasing and transmitting the mortgage advance, including dealing with any retentions;

(xii) procuring execution of the lender's mortgage deed by the borrower and any guarantor, and their signatures to the lender's forms of undertaking in relation to the use, occupation or physical state of the property;

(xiii) obtaining consents in the form required by the lender from existing or prospective occupiers of the property specified by the lender, and reporting to the lender any other occupiers notified to the solicitor by the borrower;

(xiv) advising the borrower on the terms of any document supplied by the lender for the borrower's signature;

(xv) advising any other person required to sign any document supplied by the lender on the terms of that document or, if there is a conflict of interest between that person and the borrower, advising that person on the need for separate legal advice;

(xvi) obtaining the legal transfer of the property to the borrower;

(xvii) procuring the redemption of existing mortgages on property the subject of any associated sale of which the solicitor is aware;

(xviii) ensuring the redemption or postponement of existing mortgages on the property, and registering the mortgage with the priority required by the lender;

(xix) making administrative arrangements in relation to any collateral security, such as an endowment policy;

(xx) registering the transfer and mortgage;

(xxi) giving legal advice on any matters reported on under this paragraph 3(c), and suggesting courses of action open to the lender;

(xxii) disclosing any relationship specified by the lender between the solicitor and borrower;

(xxiii) storing safely the title deeds and documents pending registration and delivery to the lender.

(d) In addition, a solicitor acting for both lender and borrower in an institutional mortgage of property to be used as a private residence only:

(i) must use the certificate of title set out in the Appendix, or as substituted from time to time by the Council with the concurrence of the Master of the Rolls, ("the approved certificate"); and

(ii) unless the lender has certified that its mortgage instructions are subject to the limitations contained in paragraphs (3)(c) and (3)(e), must notify the lender on receipt of instructions that the approved certificate will be used, and that the solicitor's duties to the lender are limited to the matters contained in the approved certificate.

(e) The terms of this rule will prevail in the event of any ambiguity in the lender's instructions, or discrepancy between the instructions and paragraph (3)(c) or the approved certificate.

Anti-avoidance

(f) A solicitor who is acting only for the borrower in an institutional mortgage of property must not accept or act upon any requirements by way of undertaking, warranty, guarantee or otherwise of the lender, the lender's solicitor or other agent which extend beyond the limitations contained in paragraph (3)(c).

Notes

(i) An "institutional mortgage" is a mortgage on standard terms, provided by an institutional lender in the normal course of its activities; and

• a "private mortgage" is any other mortgage

(ii) **A solicitor will not be in breach of paragraphs (3)(a)(iii)-(iv) or (c) if the lender has certified that its mortgage instructions are subject to the limitations set out in paragraphs (3)(c) and (e), and certifies any subsequent instructions in the same way. If there is no certification, a solicitor acting in an exclusively residential transaction must notify the lender that the approved certificate of title will be used and that the solicitor's duties to the lender will be limited accordingly (see paragraph (3)(d)(ii)). In other types of transaction, the solicitor should draw the lender's attention to the provisions of paragraphs (3)(c) and (e) and state that he or she cannot act on any instructions which extend beyond the matters contained in paragraph (3)(c).**

(iii) "Solicitor" in paragraph (3)(b)(i) means any principal in the practice (or an associated practice), and any solicitor conducting or supervising the transaction, whether or not that solicitor is a principal; and

• "immediate family" means spouse, children, parents, brothers and sisters.

(iv) The lender must be informed of the circumstances, in accordance with paragraph (3)(b) so that the lender can decide whether or not to instruct the solicitor.

(v) A lender's instructions may require a wider disclosure **of a solicitor's circumstances** than **paragraph (3)(b)** requires; and a solicitor must assess whether the circumstances give rise to a conflict. For example, there will be a conflict between lender and borrower if the solicitor becomes involved in negotiations relating to the terms of the loan. A conflict might arise from the relationship a solicitor has with the borrower - for example, if the solicitor is the borrower's creditor or debtor or the borrower's business associate or co-habitant.

(2)This amendment rule comes into effect on 1 June 1999.

Appendix
Certificate of Title

To: (Lender)
Lender's Reference or Account No:
The Borrower:
Property:
Title Number:
Mortgage Advance:
Completion Date:
Conveyancer's Name & Address:
Conveyancer's Reference:
Conveyancer's bank, sort code and account number:

WE THE CONVEYANCERS NAMED ABOVE CERTIFY as follows:

1) If you have provided any photograph(s) and/or specimen signature(s), we have checked the identity of the Borrower against them.

2) Except as otherwise disclosed to you in writing:

   i) we have investigated the title to the Property and, upon completion of the mortgage, the Borrower will have a good and marketable title to the Property and to its rights free from prior mortgages or charges and from onerous encumbrances which title will be registered with absolute title;

   ii) if you have provided a plan, we have compared the extent of the Property shown on your plan against relevant plans in the title deeds, and in our opinion there are no material discrepancies;

   iii) if the Property is leasehold the terms of the lease accord with your instructions, including any requirements you have for covenants by the Landlord and/or a management company for the insurance, repair and maintenance of the structure, exterior and common parts of any building of which the Property forms part;

   iv) the buildings insurance is in place, or will be on completion, for the sum required by you;

v) if the Property is to be purchased by the Borrower:

    a) the contract for sale provides for vacant possession on completion;

    b) the seller has owned or been the registered owner of the Property for not less than six months;

    c) we are not acting on behalf of the seller;

vi) we have made a local search (which is not more than three months old) and such other searches as are appropriate to the Property, the Borrower and any guarantor;

vii) nothing has been revealed by our searches and enquiries which would prevent the Property being used by any occupant for residential purposes;

viii) neither any principal nor any other solicitor in the practice giving this certificate nor any spouse, child, parent, brother or sister of such a person is interested in the Property (whether alone or jointly with any other) as seller, buyer or Borrower.

WE:

a) undertake, prior to use of the mortgage advance, to obtain the execution by the Borrower of a mortgage and by any guarantor of a guarantee, each in the form of the draft supplied by you, and to obtain consents in the form required by you from any existing or prospective occupier(s) of the property specified by you;

b) have made or will make such Bankruptcy, Land Registry or Land Charges Searches as may be necessary to justify certificate no. (2) (i) above;

c) will within the period of protection afforded by the searches referred to in paragraph (b) above:

    i) complete the mortgage;

    ii) arrange for stamping of the transfer if appropriate;

    iii) deliver to the Land Registry the documents necessary to register the mortgage in your favour and any relevant prior dealings;

    iv) effect any other registrations necessary to protect your interests as mortgagee;

d) will despatch to you the Charge Certificate and any other relevant deeds relating to the Property with a list of them in the form prescribed by you within ten working days of receipt by us from the Land Registry;

e) will not part with the mortgage advance (and will return it to you if required) if it shall come to our notice prior to completion that the Property will at completion be occupied in whole or in part otherwise than in accordance with your instructions;

f) will not accept instructions, except with your consent in writing, to prepare any lease or tenancy agreement relating to the Property or any part of it prior to despatch of the Charge Certificate to you;

g) will not use the mortgage advance until satisfied that any existing mortgage on property the subject of an associated sale of which we are aware, will be discharged prior to or contemporaneously with the transfer of the Property to the Borrower;

h) will notify you in writing if any matter comes to our attention before completion which would render the certificate given above untrue or inaccurate and, in those circumstances, will defer completion pending your authority to proceed and will return the mortgage advance to you if required.

OUR duties to you are limited to the matters set out in this certificate and we accept no further liability or responsibility whatsoever. The payment by you to us (by whatever means) of the mortgage advance or any part of it constitutes acceptance of this limitation and any assignment to you by the Borrower of any rights of action against us to which the Borrower may be entitled shall take effect subject to this limitation.

Subject to the above limitation we confirm that we have complied with your instructions.

Previous disclosures have been made to you under paragraph (2) above *Yes/No
New disclosures under paragraph (2) above accompany this report *Yes/No
* Delete as appropriate

SIGNED on behalf of **THE CONVEYANCERS**
NAME of Authorised Signatory
QUALIFICATION of Authorised Signatory
DATE of Signature

Questions and answers

Q1 Why is it necessary to change the rule by defining the scope of a solicitor's retainer with a lender when the solicitor is also acting for the borrower?

A1 Solicitors have traditionally been able to act for both lender and borrower because their duties to the lender were restricted to matters of title where the lender's and borrower's interests coincide. Over the last few years lenders have increasingly required solicitors to undertake tasks and give assurances on mattes which go beyond the work normally required of solicitors by lenders. This has led to an increased risk of conflict between the interests of lender and borrower.

Q2 What about the current restrictions?

A2 These remain unchanged:

- acting for both lender and borrower is never allowed if there is a conflict of interest – paragraph 3(a)(i);

- acting for both lender and borrower is never allowed on the grant of a private mortgage of land at arm's length – paragraph 3(a)(ii);

- a solicitor must disclose to an institutional lender certain relationships with the borrower (eg solicitor is borrower's sister), and if solicitor will be acting for seller, buyer and lender – paragraph 3(b) and notes (iii)–(v).

Q3 Assuming there is no conflict of interest, is it still possible to act for both the lender and the borrower in an institutional mortgage?

A3 Yes, but the new Rule 6(3) imposes certain safeguards to reduce the risk of a conflict of interest arising:

- the lender's instructions must not extend beyond the limitations contained in paragraphs 3(c) and 3(e) – this applies to all types of transaction, residential, commercial or mixed;

- in addition, the approved certificate of title set out in the Appendix to Rule 6(3) must be used for exclusively residential transactions – paragraph 3(d).

Q4 How am I to ensure that the mortgage instructions comply with the rule?

A4 It is envisaged that lenders will certify that their mortgage instructions do not extend beyond the limitations set out in the rule and, if that is the case, the solicitor need take no further action – note (ii).

Q5   What if the lender's mortgage instructions are not certified?

A5   The following steps should be taken:

- in a residential transaction the solicitor must notify the lender on receipt of instructions that the approved certificate of title will be used, and that the solicitor's duties to the lender are limited to the matters contained in the approved certificate – paragraph (3)(d) and note (ii).

- for other types of transaction, the solicitor should notify the lender that the solicitor cannot act on any instructions which extend beyond the matters contained in the rule – note (ii).

Q6   What if I am acting for the borrower only but the lender's solicitor requires me to give undertakings which relate to matters outside those listed in paragraph (3)(c)?

A6   You must decline to accept or act upon any such requirements – paragraph (3)(f).

12 Solicitors' Obligations when Advising Guarantors and Sureties

Introduction

Most couples whether married or not own their home jointly. Banks and lending institutions often require a charge over that home as security for their business lending. The business is often owned or run by just one of the home owners. It often makes commercial sense to use the collateral in the home as security for bank borrowing. Sometimes it is the parents who own the home and the adult children who need to borrow from a bank. All these situations now present themselves to practitioners on a daily basis. The banks want to protect themselves from the possibility that the courts will not enforce the security. Practitioners want to ensure that the surety has full advice and is not being forced into agreeing to sign away their home. Unfortunately, many practitioners have not realised the importance of strong clear advice in these circumstances and many charges have been routinely signed without proper advice being given.

Barclays Bank plc v *O'Brien* [1993] 4 All ER 417 House of Lords (Lords Templeman, Lowry, Browne-Wilkinson, Slynn of Hadley and Woolf)

The House of Lords agreed that there was a class of sureties that may need special protection. These included spouses and parents. In these cases the lending institutions must take reasonable steps to ensure that the surety understands what is being signed and what the true nature of the transaction really is. The surety must not have undue influence exerted on them and must freely consent to the transaction. The lender would discharge their obligations if the surety was warned of the amount of the potential liability and of the risks involved and told to take independent legal advice. This has led to lending institutions sending sureties to solicitors for advice as a matter of course before agreeing to the loan facility. Many institutions also insist on the solicitor witnessing the signature of the surety and confirming that proper advice has been given.

The House of Lords decided that prima facie, it is not in the best interests of a wife to stand surety for her husband's debts and that if she does, the husband may have committed a legal or equitable wrong, entitling the wife to have the transaction set aside.

A number of subsequent cases expanded on some general principles:

- The lender cannot be expected to look behind the advice given by the solicitor to the surety even if the same solicitor is acting for the lender.
- The lender must make sure that the surety has received independent advice before the loan is completed.
- When a solicitor acts for both the lender and surety any knowledge acquired in his capacity as adviser to the surety is not attributed to the lender.
- When the solicitor is advising the surety the solicitor is acting for the surety not the lender.
- The burden of proving that all the obligations have been complied with rests with the lender.

Royal Bank of Scotland v Etridge and Associated Cases [1998] 4 All ER 705 Court of Appeal (Stuart-Smith, Millett and Morritt LJJ)

There were six cases used by Court of Appeal to explain in detail what the responsibilities of the lender were to ensure that the surety was acting freely and with independent advice. They also explained the responsibilities of the solicitor in giving advice.

Held
- Undue influence

  The solicitor's duty was to satisfy himself that the surety was free from undue influence and could enter into the transaction free from such influence. If there was undue influence, the solicitor must advise the surety not to sign. If the surety insists on proceeding, the solicitor must refuse to act further and inform the lender that he is no longer acting. He should not inform the lender exactly why he has withdrawn from the matter. If the solicitor is satisfied that there is no undue influence then he can continue to advise on the merits of the transaction. The advice must include a full explanation of the potential liability of the surety, in other words an honest evaluation of the worst case scenario. The solicitor should negotiate with the lender and not assume that the offer is on a take-it-or-leave-it basis. The solicitor can act for both the husband and the wife although it is difficult to imagine a situation where there is no conflict of interests between husband and wife. The advice must include a warning that if the marriage came to an end the wife's rights to recover her share of the matrimonial home may be jeopardised.

- The position between the wife and the lender

  It had been suggested in *O'Brien* that the lender must have a personal interview with the wife to discover whether the wife had an equity which was capable of setting aside the transaction. Few lenders wanted to adhere to this and preferred to send the surety to a solicitor. The Code of Banking Practice confirmed it was sufficient to advise the surety to obtain independent legal advice and this was supported by the Court of Appeal in *Etridge*.

- Effect of legal advice

  Stuart-Smith LJ said:

  'It was highly undesirable that the validity of such transactions should depend on fine distinctions in the wording of the instructions to solicitors or the certificates they gave ... It followed from the need to avoid subtle distinctions that their Lordships attached no importance to the fact that the solicitor might not provide the bank with a full or adequate confirmation that he had followed his instructions. Where the bank had asked him to explain the transaction to the wife and confirm that she appeared to understand it, the bank was not put on enquiry by the fact that the solicitor had confirmed that he had explained the transaction to her but not that she appeared to understand it.'

  The court found that where the solicitor fails to confirm that he has explained the transaction fully to the wife, the bank is on risk. However if the advice has actually been given, the bank is not affected by notice of the wife's equity. This is a somewhat surprising approach by the Court of Appeal. Surely if the bank is on notice of the risk of undue influence or misrepresentation and has not investigated further it must still have notice of the wife's equity.

  The court added a further protection for a wife:

  'If the bank was in possession of material information which was not available to the solicitor, or if the transaction was one which no competent solicitor could properly advise the wife to enter, the availability of legal advice was insufficient to avoid the bank being fixed with constructive notice.'

Practical steps to take when advising a surety

The courts have placed a great deal of responsibility and liability on the shoulders of the solicitor. Many practitioners routinely advised sureties without realising the huge potential liability they faced. In the light of *O'Brien* and *Etridge* the practitioners' approach must change. The following steps must be taken to ensure that no liability will rest on the shoulders of the practitioner.

- Do not act for the wife if you are also acting for the husband or the husband's business. The risk of conflict of interest is too high.
- Open a separate file in respect of the advice being given to the surety. The surety will be the client, not the bank.
- Interview the wife by herself.
- If there is any evidence of undue influence or misrepresentation, advise the wife not to proceed.
- If the wife wishes to proceed then indicate that you can no longer act for her. Inform the bank that you have given certain advice and have withdrawn from the matter.
- Make full and detailed attendance notes at all times.
- If you are satisfied that there is no undue influence or misrepresentation then explain the nature and effect of the transaction. Ensure that the wife understands both.
- Ensure that she wishes to continue with the transaction. Advise her that she is under no obligation to enter into it.
- Advise her that she is not obliged to accept the standard documentation or the suggested maximum liability. Offer to negotiate with the bank a less onerous obligation.
- Advice must include the effect of the charge on a dissolution of marriage.
- Advice must include an analysis of the purpose behind the loan and the likely ability of the husband or the husband's business to service the loan. If this information is not available then the wife must be asked if she wishes further investigation to be carried out before she proceeds with the transaction. It may be necessary to involve an accountant to advise on the viability of the loan.
- Go through the documentation very carefully and explain it in layman's terms.

- If the charge is for an unlimited amount explain the full consequences. Explore the possibility of limiting the amount of the surety.
- Suggest the surety spends a few days reflecting on the transaction.
- Follow any guidelines issued by the lending institution.
- If the surety does not have a good understanding of English, insist on using an interpreter.
- Enquire whether any promises have been given to the surety by the creditor.
- Check whether any other persons have an interest in the home, eg an elderly parent.
- Write a letter to the client confirming the steps you have taken and the advice you have given.

Do not accept instructions unless you are prepared to carry out all these steps. The client must be warned that the likely costs of this advice will be substantial in the light of recent cases that have increased the responsibilities of the solicitor.

Further reading

Guarantors: A Practical Handbook for Giving Independent Legal Advice, Laird Tennent

Index

LAW IN PRACTICE SERIES

from

Old Bailey Press
The New Publishers for Practitioners

This text is part of the new and dynamic *Law in Practice Series*.

The series comprises a range of *Concise Texts* dealing with recent developments in key mainstream areas of legal practice and providing a pathway through some of the more complex areas of contemporary legal practice (eg residential tenancies, financial services).

The *Concise Texts* have a number of features which give them a dynamism relevant to contemporary practice including the following:

- Topical, relevant and up-to-date
- Written for practitioners
- Clear and direct writing style
- Evaluative commentary
- Authors with relevant practice experience
- Support materials for Holborn College CPD courses
- Time-efficient reading
- Outstanding value for money

Further, the *Law in Practice Series* includes a number of specialist texts on some of the fast-emerging areas of contemporary legal practice.

Full details of the series is set out below.

Concise Texts	ISBN	Price
Commercial Property	1-85836-283-0	£6.95
Employment Law	1-85836-291-1	£6.95
European Union Law	1-85836-297-0	£6.95
Identifying Current Residential Tenancies	1-85836-288-1	£6.95
Introduction to Financial Services	1-85836-287-3	£6.95
Residential Tenancies	1-85836-086-2	£6.95

To complete your order, please fill in the form below:

Books required	ISBN	Quantity	Price	Cost
		Postage		
		TOTAL		

For UK, add 10% postage and packing.
For Europe, add 15% postage and packing.

ORDERING

By telephone to: Mail Order at 0171 385 3377, with your credit card to hand

By fax to: 0171 381 3377 (giving your credit card details)

By post to: Old Bailey Press, 200 Greyhound Road, London W14 9RY

When ordering by post, please enclose full payment by cheque or banker's draft, or complete the credit card details below.

We aim to despatch your books within three working days of receiving your order.

Name

Address

Postcode   Telephone

Total value of order, including postage: £

I enclose a cheque/banker's draft for the above sum, or

Charge my ☐ Access/Mastercard ☐ Visa ☐ American Express

Card number ☐☐☐☐ ☐☐☐☐ ☐☐☐☐ ☐☐☐☐

Expiry date ☐☐☐☐

Signature: ....Date: ....